Auditing, Governance & Ethics

ACIS 3414

| PEARSON COLLECTIONS |

PEARSON

Cover Art: Courtesy of Photodisc/Getty Images

Pearson Learning Solutions, 501 Boylston Street, Suite 900, Boston, MA 02116

A Pearson Education Company
www.pearsoned.com

PEARSON

ISBN 10: 1323729968

ISBN 13: 9781323729960

Printed in the USA

1 17

Table of Contents

Accountants as Communicators

The ability to communicate effectively, whether through speaking or writing, is essential to success in the accounting profession and in the business world in general.[1] Writing and speaking, interpersonal skills, leadership skills, and the ability to think critically and to listen carefully are sometimes referred to as "soft skills," as opposed to the "hard skills" of technical knowledge and ability. The major differences among competitors may often be found in the degree to which employees have mastered writing, speaking, and other non-technical skills.

Soft skills are generally regarded as the key to business success and more important than technical accounting skills. One highly successful accountant has pointed out the importance of both writing and thinking:

> Some of the smartest accountants I have ever known are not the ones who knew standards backwards and forwards, but the ones that knew how to write and think.[2]

These skills are especially important in today's global environment. According to the International Accounting Education Standards Board (IAESB), successful accountants must be able to "present, discuss, report and defend views effectively through formal, informal, written and spoken communication; and . . . listen and read effectively."[3]

As you can see, to achieve your career goals in accounting, you may need to improve your communication skills. The American Institute of Certified Public Accountants (AICPA) believes that communication skills are now and will continue to be as important as professional knowledge, analysis and organization skills, technological skills, and research skills—all of which are essential for entry-level accountants (Figure 1). Among the personal attributes listed by the AICPA for competency in public accounting is "effective business writing." An AICPA report says that the writing of entry-level professionals should demonstrate standard grammar, appropriate style and tone, logical organization, clarity, and conciseness.[4]

FIGURE 1 Knowledge and Skills Required of Entry-Level CPAs

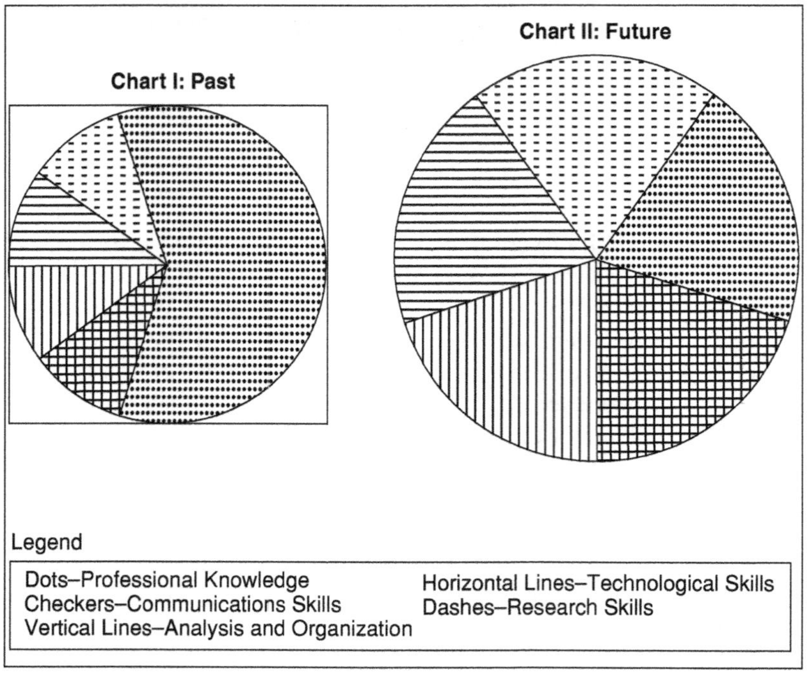

Source: American Institute of Certified Public Accountants, Briefing Paper No. 2, *Computerizing the Uniform CPA Examination—Issues, Strategies, and Policies: An Update*, 5 March 2001.

Effective writing skills are essential for accountants in all areas of professional practice, including managerial accounting. The IMA (formerly known as the Institute of Management Accountants) has stated that "written communication is a critically important skill set for the management accountant and for the effective functioning of accounting and finance teams."[5]

So to be successful as well as competent, accountants must be good communicators, showing that they can use words effectively. Many colleges and universities now stress effective writing in accounting coursework. The AICPA evaluates candidates' writing skills on the CPA exam,[6] and the IMA evaluates writing skills on the CMA exam.[7]

Unfortunately, some students and accountants lack the skills they need to be effective communicators. Accounting firms are on record as being dissatisfied with the communication skills of entry-level accountants,[8] and a high percentage of accounting firms have reported poor writing skills as one reason for job terminations.[9]

Accountants need communication skills to get a good job and to keep that job after they are hired. Of course, "communication skills" is a broad area that includes formal and informal oral presentations, interpersonal communication, reading, listening, and skills in other related areas, including the ability to think carefully and critically. Ethical issues can also affect communication, both what accountants say and how they say it. Because this text is primarily about writing, we will now look at some of the documents accountants write on the job.

WHAT DO ACCOUNTANTS WRITE?

In every type of accounting practice, writing is an essential part of the job. Whether in public accounting, management accounting, not-for-profit accounting, or government accounting,[10] and whether specializing in tax, auditing, systems, or some other area, accountants write almost every day.

Examples in three specialized areas—tax, auditing, and systems—suggest a few of the many occasions that require accountants to write.

Tax accountants in accounting firms often write memos to other members of the firm that describe the results of their research. These memos become part of the clients' files. A tax accountant might also write a letter advising the client about the best way to handle a tax problem. Tax accountants must also write letters to the Internal Revenue Service (IRS) on behalf of clients, and occasionally may even write a judicial brief.

Auditors write memos to be included in a client's audit files that describe the work done on the audit. They may also write memos to their colleagues to request advice or to report research results. After the audit engagement, auditors may write advisory letters to management that suggest ways to improve accounting and internal control procedures.

Systems specialists write documents for readers with varying degrees of computer expertise. They may write a beginners' guide on how to use a software package or a highly technical report on a complex accounting system application. They may also write a narrative description of an accounting information system, as we will see later in this chapter.

No matter what their specialty, all accountants write memos to their supervisors, subordinates, and co-workers to request or provide information. They also write letters to clients, agencies, and a variety of other readers.

Technical reports and memos, both formal and informal, are also important ways in which accountants communicate. For instance, an accountant working for a corporation might write a report for management on alternative accounting treatments for a particular kind of business transaction. An accountant working for an accounting or business services firm might write a technical memo on how best to handle a client's unusual accounting problem.

Yet another kind of writing prepared by accountants is the narrative portion of financial statements. Footnote disclosures communicate information that users may need to interpret the statements accurately. Unfortunately, the meaning of some footnote disclosures is not always clear to many financial statement readers. Several years ago, the Securities and Exchange Commission (SEC) issued a "plain English" disclosure rule requiring companies filing registration statements to write those statements in "plain English" so that readers would find them easier to understand. The rule enumerates several principles of "plain English," including the use of short sentences and clear, concise language.[11]

Not all professional writing appears on paper. Email is nearly universal, and other forms of electronic communication have become increasingly important in recent years.

To be effective, letters, memos, emails, reports, and other business documents must be well written. How will clients react if, after reading a letter from their CPA, they are still confused about their income tax problem? How will management or one's supervisors react to a report that is poorly organized and hard to follow?

HOW WELL DO ACCOUNTANTS WRITE?

Earlier we noted that many entry-level accountants lack adequate writing skills, even though the ability to write well is essential for success in the business world. Some people believe the problem is getting worse, in part because we have become an online society in which a large part of everyday communication occurs via email and other forms of electronic communication. Electronic communication often emphasizes brevity over completeness, clarity, or attention to style. Therefore, we are being conditioned to use a type of writing that is not effective in many business situations. Yet even email and other forms of electronic communication can be written effectively.

WHAT MAKES WRITING WORK?

What is good writing? The list of tips for writers in Figure 2 summarizes many qualities of effective business writing, including the writing done by accountants. Let's examine these tips in a little more detail.

The first tip concerns the *content* of the document. You must know what you are talking about, and the information you give should be accurate and relevant. The second tip is *critical thinking.* You must analyze the issues with which you are dealing, including the questions and concerns of your readers. Can the issues be resolved in more than one way? If so, you will have to evaluate the alternatives carefully.

FIGURE 2 Tips for the Effective Writer

1. *Content:* Be sure that the accounting content is correct and complete. Have you addressed all relevant accounting issues?
2. *Critical Thinking:* Think carefully and critically about the issues with which you're dealing. Anticipate questions and objections your readers might raise.
3. *Appropriateness for Readers:* Write the document with a particular reader in mind. Check that issues are discussed on a level the reader can understand. For most documents, it is better to focus on practical, explicit information and advice related to the case you are discussing rather than general accounting theory.
4. *Conciseness:* Write as concisely as possible, given the reader's needs and the issues to be addressed.
5. *Clarity:* Develop a style that is clear and readable. Choose words that convey your meaning with precision and clarity.
6. *Coherence:* Structure the document so that it is coherent. The organization should be logical and the train of thought easy to follow. Summarize main ideas near the beginning of the document, and begin each paragraph with a topic sentence.
7. *Revision:* Revise the document so that it is polished and professional. It should be free of all spelling errors and typos; grammatical errors should not detract from the message.

The third tip for effective writing is *to write appropriately for your readers*. Your writing should be suitable for readers in several ways: It should be written on a level they understand and find meaningful, and it should anticipate and answer their questions.

The fourth tip is *conciseness*. Say what needs to be said in as few words as possible. To keep your writing concise, avoid digressions, unnecessary repetition, and wordiness.

Clarity is the next tip. Write as simply as possible, using words and phrases with which the reader is familiar. To improve the clarity of your writing, choose words that mean precisely what you intend so that your sentences convey only one meaning: the meaning you want to convey. Well-structured sentences also contribute to clear writing.

Coherence is the logical, orderly relationship of ideas. Coherent writing is, simply, writing that is well organized. The flow of thought is easy to follow, and important ideas stand out. To write coherently, you must carefully think through the ideas you want to convey. The ideas must be arranged logically and then written in a way readers can comprehend. Coherence is the sixth tip for effective writers.

The final tip is to *revise* your writing so that it is polished and professional. Documents should look attractive and be free of grammatical and mechanical errors.

EFFECTIVE WRITING: AN EXAMPLE

Accountants are called on to write many kinds of documents. One such document is the narrative description of an accounting information system (AIS). Figure 3 is an example of such a narrative description, in this case the payroll processing system of a hypothetical company, S&S, a small retail business owned by Scott and Susan. This description illustrates many of the characteristics of effective writing introduced here.

If you read the description, you will notice that it is organized logically, following the steps of the payroll process, so that the narrative is *coherent*. That is, readers will be able to understand how this system functions. Paragraphs are short and easy to follow. Sentences are *clear* and *concise*. The language is *correct*—written following the conventions of Standard English. The document is also written at a level *appropriate* to the readers, whom we assume to be the owners, managers, and other professionals who work with the payroll system at S&S.

YOU CAN BECOME A GOOD WRITER

With all this talk about the importance of good writing to a successful career in accounting, you may feel overwhelmed or discouraged. Many people believe that they can never become good writers.

A word of encouragement is in order. Virtually anyone who succeeds in college work has the education and the skills to become at least an adequate writer, and probably even a good one. Problems with writing are often the result of two factors, both of which can be corrected: lack of adequate training in writing skills, and lack of self-confidence.

Let's address the latter problem—the poor image some people have of themselves as writers. One reason to be optimistic about your writing ability is that you've already learned quite a bit about how to write from English courses and other writing classes, as well as from personal experience. Most people are better writers than they realize. They have the potential to become even more effective after they've mastered a few additional strategies. As you read this text, note the techniques and principles you already use in your writing. Don't lose sight of your strengths while you work to improve the areas that could be better.

Another reason you should be able to write well as an accountant is that you will be writing about topics you understand and find interesting. If you have had unpleasant experiences with writing in courses other than accounting, the problem may have been that you were writing about topics you weren't particularly interested in or didn't

FIGURE 3 Narrative Description of Payroll Processing at S&S[12]

When employees are hired, they complete a new-employee form. When a change to an employee's payroll status occurs, such as a raise or a change in the number of exemptions, the human resources department completes an employee change form. A copy of these forms is sent to payroll. These forms are used to create or update the records in the employee/payroll file and are then stored in the file. Employee records are stored alphabetically.

Some S&S employees are paid a salary, but most are hourly workers who record their time on time cards. At the end of each pay period, department managers send the time cards to the payroll department. The payroll clerk uses the time card data, data from the employee file (such as pay rate and annual salary), and the appropriate tax tables to prepare a two-part check for each employee. The clerk also prepares a two-part payroll register showing gross pay, deductions, and net pay for each employee. The clerk updates the employee file to reflect each employee's current earnings. The original copy of the employee paychecks is forwarded to Susan. The payroll register is forwarded to the accounts payable clerk. The time cards and the duplicate copies of the payroll register and paychecks are stored by date in the payroll file.

Every pay period, the payroll clerk uses the data in the employee/payroll file to prepare a payroll summary report for Susan so that she can control and monitor labor expenses. This report is forwarded to Susan, with the original copies of the employee paychecks.

Every month, the payroll clerk uses the data in the employee/payroll file to prepare a two-part tax report. The original is forwarded to the accounts payable clerk, and the duplicate is added to the tax records in the payroll file. The accounts payable clerk uses the tax report to prepare a two-part check for taxes and a two-part cash disbursements voucher. The tax report and the original copy of each document are forwarded to Susan. The duplicates are stored by date in the accounts payable file.

The accounts payable clerk uses the payroll register to prepare a two-part check for the total amount of the employee payroll and a two-part disbursements voucher. The original copy of each document is forwarded to Susan, and the payroll register and the duplicates are stored by date in the accounts payable file.

Susan reviews each packet of information she receives, approves it, and signs the checks. She forwards the cash disbursements vouchers to Ashton, the tax reports and payments to the appropriate governmental agency, the payroll check to the bank, and the employee checks to the employees. She files the payroll report chronologically.

Ashton uses the payroll tax and the payroll check cash disbursement vouchers to update the general ledger. He then cancels the journal voucher by marking it "posted" and files it numerically.

feel qualified to discuss. When you write about subjects you like and understand, it's much easier to write clearly and persuasively.

Finally, you may find it much easier to do the kind of writing recommended in this text because it is simple, direct writing. Some people believe that they must write in long, complicated sentences filled with difficult, "impressive" vocabulary. In fact, just the opposite is true: Effective business writing is written as simply as possible. It is therefore easier to do.

WRITING AND OTHER FORMS OF COMMUNICATION

Writing is only one of several forms of communication, along with such skills as reading, listening, speaking, and interpersonal communication. In fact, all these forms of communication work together to determine how well a person gives and receives information. Let's look at how reading, listening, and speaking skills can help you improve your writing.

Reading

Reading affects writing in several ways. Often you will write a memo or letter in response to a written communication from someone else. In public practice, for example, you might write a letter to clients to answer questions they have posed in a letter to your firm. The ability to read the earlier correspondence carefully is essential to an effective response.

Careful reading is also important when you research accounting literature as background for the documents you write. The tax code, government regulations, financial accounting standards, articles in professional journals, and *The Wall Street Journal* are examples of the material you must read to stay informed on accounting issues and procedures. You will need to understand this material and be able to apply it to particular situations.

You will also read information circulated and stored within your own firm or company, such as client files and memos or emails from colleagues. Reading this material carefully will provide many of the insights and facts you need to deal effectively with situations for which you are responsible.

Thus, careful reading, with an understanding of important ideas and key facts, can contribute to effective writing.

Listening

Along with reading, the ability to listen carefully determines how well you receive information from others. On the job, you interact with colleagues, supervisors, subordinates, or clients; at school, you interact with professors and other students. Listening carefully to these people provides important information you can use as the basis of your writing. Listening gives you facts about projects you are working on, along with insights into other people's expectations and concerns.

In many situations, listening skills contribute to effective writing. Instructions given by the professor in class, interviews with clients, requests from supervisors, and phone conversations with colleagues are a few examples. In all these situations, attentive listening is necessary to hear what people are saying. It's often a good idea to take notes and, when necessary, ask questions for clarification or additional information.

Careful listening to what others say is often a key ingredient in effective writing. By listening carefully, you learn much about what others know about a situation, what their concerns are, and what they expect from you.

Speaking

Oral communication is one of the soft skills we mentioned earlier as important to success in the accounting profession. Writing and speaking will often overlap in your professional activities. Informally, you may have meetings and conversations to discuss reports or memos you've written. You may use what you've written as the basis for formal oral presentations before a group. You might make a presentation to a board of directors, senior managers, or members of a professional organization.

WRITING AND PROBLEM SOLVING

The nation's largest public accounting firms are unanimous in calling for improved communication skills for those entering the profession. These firms also identify problem-solving skills as essential to successful accounting practice:

> Individuals seeking to be successful in the diverse world of public accounting must be able to use creative problem-solving skills in a consultative process. They must be able to solve diverse and unstructured problems in unfamiliar settings. They must be able to comprehend an unfocused set of facts; identify and, if possible, anticipate problems; and find acceptable solutions.[13]

Problem solving requires many skills, such as identifying key issues, researching relevant literature, and thinking critically and analytically. At each step of the problem-solving process, writing can help you reach sound conclusions.

You can generate ideas on a topic by writing down what you know about that topic, as well as what you have yet to find out. The act of writing about a subject can actually help you clarify your thinking. As one wit put it, "How do I know what I think until I see what I say?" There's more truth in this quip than might at first be apparent. Research into how people think and learn has shown that writers often generate ideas and improve their insights into a subject as they write down their thoughts.

Writing can help you solve problems in other ways as well. For example, as you research accounting literature, you take notes. You might also write requests to other people for additional information you need to solve the problem.

Writing that you use to solve problems and make decisions is writing for yourself. After the problems have been solved, or at least clearly defined, you can put your insights and conclusions into writing that will help you and others make decisions. Writing, problem solving, and decision making are often inseparable, interactive processes that are essential to the practice of accounting.

WRITING AND CRITICAL THINKING

We've seen that problem solving and decision making, like writing and other forms of communication, are significant parts of an accountant's job. But before you can solve a problem or make a decision, you need to think carefully and critically about the issues at hand.

What is critical thinking? It can be defined as fair, open-minded thinking that asks appropriate questions and considers all relevant information before reaching a conclusion. A critical thinker considers a situation from multiple points of view and evaluates the pros and cons of an argument before reaching a conclusion. Critical thinkers are careful to avoid errors, or fallacies, in their thinking and analyses.

Critical thinking and effective writing go hand in hand: As you take notes and write down your ideas about an accounting problem, the issues and alternative solutions will become clearer. This critical thinking becomes important as you prepare to write the final document.

COMMUNICATIONS AND ETHICS

Accounting communication, including writing, may involve ethical considerations as well as critical thinking and problem solving. In fact, these three processes—analyzing ethical and other accounting issues, thinking critically, and solving problems—are often essential components of effective communication.

Ethics may be defined broadly as the standards we use to determine what is right and wrong—a set of moral principles or values that govern how we act. We learn these ethical principles in a variety of ways, from our families, religious communities, schools, or in general from the society of which we are a part. Professional people, including accountants, also acquire ethical standards as part of their professional training.

Accountants must adhere to very high ethical standards as they perform their professional responsibilities. CPAs must follow reporting rules established by the SEC and other governmental agencies, and they must adhere to ethical standards established by nongovernmental entities such as the Financial Accounting Standards Board (FASB) and the AICPA. In fact, the AICPA's Code of Professional Ethics is a major source of ethical standards for all accounting professionals, not just CPAs. Management accountants also adhere to ethical requirements established by the IMA, as well as by federal, state, and local laws. Individual firms and corporations may also have ethical codes for their employees.

Legal requirements and codes of professional conduct provide standards of ethical behavior for accountants as they perform their professional responsibilities. Yet these laws and codes alone may not always provide enough guidance for specific ethical dilemmas. Accountants sometimes face situations for which ready-made answers are not available. When you are faced with such a dilemma, you will need to think critically about the issues in light of your own personal ethical standards in order to make an ethical decision. Remember, too, that there may be a gap between what is legal and what is ethical. For many years, discrimination against ethnic minorities and women was legal in this country, but such discrimination was never ethical.

Ethical considerations often affect the way we communicate in a professional situation, whether orally or in writing. Remember that accounting is a process of measuring and reporting financial information. Ethical issues can relate to what we say and how we say it. The AICPA's Code of Professional Ethics requires that its members report all the information needed for a user of the information to make a reasonable decision; the Code also requires that financial data not be misrepresented. Thus, information must be reported in an honest, reasonably complete manner. Moreover, the information must be communicated clearly so that users can understand it. Accuracy, clarity, and completeness are all qualities of the ethical communication of accounting information.

Ethics also affects the attitude with which we regard other people, whether the public at large, our clients, or colleagues and coworkers. An important principle here is that other people deserve to be treated with courtesy and respect. Relevant ethical considerations include writing with a courteous tone, the respectful use of titles and pronouns, and the need to write clear and concise documents so that readers can find the information they need as quickly as possible. Analyzing readers' interests and needs is also an essential step in the writing process. You need to decide what information to provide, and how to provide it in a way that not only adheres to professional and legal standards, but also shows respect for the people who will use the information.

CONCLUSION

To be a successful accountant, you must master many skills. You must understand and be able to apply accounting principles, of course, but you must also be able to think critically and ethically and to communicate effectively. A competent, ethical accountant who is also a critical thinker and an effective communicator usually is rewarded with professional success.

EXERCISES

Exercise 1 [General]

Consider the writing you find in one or two articles in *The Wall Street Journal* or the business section of another major newspaper or magazine. How effective, or ineffective, do you find the writing? If you have trouble reading or understanding what you read, is the problem due to ineffective writing? If you find the material understandable and interesting to read, what qualities of the writing contribute to this effectiveness? You might consider the Tips for Effective Writing in Figure 2 as the basis of your evaluation.

Exercise 2 [Financial]

Look at some published corporate SEC Forms 10-K or annual reports for the most recent year and evaluate the financial statement disclosures they contain. Find examples of disclosures that are not written as clearly or concisely as they could be and rewrite them to be more clear and concise. Share your results with the class and discuss them. (Hint: You can access many 10-Ks and annual reports on the Internet by following the links to listed companies at the New York Stock Exchange (NYSE) Web site at https://nyse.nyx.com.)

Exercise 3 [General]

Prepare a written report on why the SEC is so concerned that corporations use "plain English" in their filings and what it is doing about the issue. Among the materials you consult, be sure to look at the following SEC publications, but do not limit your sources to just these:

- *A Plain English Handbook: How to Create Clear SEC Disclosure Documents* at www.sec.gov/news/extra/handbook.htm
- *Updated Staff Legal Bulletin No. 7* at www.sec.gov/interps/legal/cfslb7a.htm
- *Plain English Disclosure Final Rules* at www.sec.gov/rules/final/33-7497.txt

Exercise 4 [General]

Research the topic of "soft skills" and prepare an article for your school's newspaper on their definition and importance in the accounting and business world.

Exercise 5 [Ethics]

Do you believe ethical considerations are an important part of an accountant's professional responsibilities? Why or why not? Think about this question, and then write notes according to the following outline. Use only the sections of the outline that are relevant to your position on this issue.

1. Ethical considerations are important to accountants because: (list your reasons)
2. Ethical considerations are not very important to accountants because: (list your reasons)
3. Accountants find guidance in making ethical decisions from the following sources: (list the sources you find)

Exercise 6 [Managerial]

Management Accounting Quarterly (MAQ) contains articles related to managerial accounting. Search a few recent editions to find an article that may interest you. Critique the writing using each of the Tips for Effective Writing in Figure 2. How effective or ineffective do you find the writing? Does the writing style contribute to your understanding of the article? Why or why not? (You can access MAQ on line at http://www.imanet.org/resources_and_publications/management_accounting_quarterly.aspx. Access is on a subscription basis, so you may have to gain access through your school's library.)

Exercise 7 [Auditing]

AccountingWEB (www.accountingweb.com) contains articles related to many areas in accounting including auditing. Search *AccountingWEB* to find an auditing article that may interest you. Critique the writing using each of the Tips for Effective Writing in Figure 2. How effective or ineffective do you find the writing? Does the writing style contribute to your understanding of the article? Why or why not?

Exercise 8 [Systems]

Smart Brief (www.smartbrief.com/industry/accounting) is a source for newsletters that publish articles on various topics. One of these newsletters is *InfoTech Update*, which addresses topics relating to information technology in accounting. Search *InfoTech Update* on *Smart Brief* to find an information technology article that may interest you. Critique the writing using each of the Tips for Effective Writing in Figure 2. How effective or ineffective do you find the writing? Does the writing style contribute to your understanding of the article? Why or why not?

Exercise 9 [Tax]

Journal of Accountancy (published by the American Institute of Certified Public Accountants) and *The CPA Journal* (published by the New York State Society of CPAs) publish articles on many topics of interest to practicing accountants. Search these publications to find an article on tax that may interest you. Critique the writing using each of the Tips for Effective Writing in Figure 2. How effective or ineffective do you find the writing? Does the writing style contribute to your understanding of the article? Why or why not?

Exercise 10 [International]

The International Journal of Accounting, published by the University of Illinois, contains articles explaining international accounting practices. Search this publication to find an article on international accounting that may interest you. Critique the writing using each of the Tips for Effective Writing in Figure 2. How effective or ineffective do you find the writing? Does the writing style contribute to your understanding of the article? Why or why not?

Exercise 11 [General]

The chair of the accounting department at your school has asked you to address beginning accounting students at an orientation session. The topic of your presentation is to be "A Competitive Edge: The Importance of Writing Skills for Accountants." Your purpose is to convince the students to take the need for good writing skills seriously.

Write an outline you can use as a basis for your presentation. As steps in preparing your outline, follow these guidelines:

- Analyze your audience for this presentation. How will you present your topic so that they find it meaningful and interesting?
- Think critically about the objections your audience might raise to your arguments. How will you respond to their objections?
- What material will you include in your presentation? Remember to anticipate your audience's objections, and the way you will respond. Also remember to arrange your ideas in a logical order.
- Practice and present your talk. Your instructor may ask you to make your presentation in class. As an alternative, you may ask a few friends to listen to your presentation.

Exercise 12 [General]

Assume that the talk you presented for Exercise 11 was very successful. In fact, the chair of your accounting department has asked you to write an article based on your talk for the departmental website, which is available to all accounting majors.

Write the article.

Exercise 13 [Current Professional Issues]

The AICPA has listed fraud control as an emerging professional issue. Read what the institute has to say about "Managing the Business Risk of Fraud" at http://www.acfe.com/uploadedFiles/ACFE_Website/Content/documents/managing-business-risk.pdf. Critique the writing using each of the Tips for Effective Writing in Figure 2. How effective or ineffective do you find the writing? Does the writing style contribute to your understanding of the article? Why or why not?

NOTES

1. This is true not only in accounting but also in almost any business occupation including the areas of finance, marketing, and consulting. As pointed out in an article in *Business Week*, even new employees in these areas may have to prepare long reports or presentations as well as shorter forms of writing on the job. See Julie Gordon, "Memo to Students: Writing Skills Matter," *Business Week*, 26 April 2006. http://www.businessweek.com/stories/2006-04-25/memo-to-students-writing-skills-matter (9 April 2013).
2. Don Pfluger of CPA and business advisory firm Gallina as quoted in Bill Carlino, "The new breed of auditors," *accountingTODAY*, 1 May 2012. http://www.accountingtoday.com/ato_issues/26_5/Auditor-Landes-AICPA-Enron-Worldcom-audit-62448-1.html (9 April 2013).
3. International Accounting Education Standards Board (IAESB), *IES 3: Professional Skills and General Education.* (New York: IAESB, 2004), pars. 13, 17; reprinted in *Handbook of International Education Pronouncements 2010 Edition.* (New York, IAESB, 2010), 48–49.
4. American Institute of Certified Public Accountants, Invitation to Comment, *AICPA Competency Model for the New Finance Professional.* (New York: AICPA, 7 October 1997), 5.
5. William Cordes, Director of Exam Administration for the IMA, personal email (15 May 2013).
6. The Business Environment and Concepts (BEC) section of the exam contains three written communications tasks. See "A Guide to CBT-e: The New 2011 Uniform CPA Examination," https://www.aicpa.org/BecomeACPA/CPAExam/ForCandidates/HowToPrepare/DownloadableDocuments/New_2011_CPA_exam_guide_to_CBTe.pdf (9 April 2013).

7. The exam contains two 30-minute essay questions on each of the two parts of the exam. See "Become a CMA®," www.imanet.org/cma_certification/become_a_cma.aspx (10 May 2013).
8. *The Wall Street Journal*, 16 July 1986, "Words Count," 1.
9. Alan A. Cherry and Lucy A. Wilson, "A Study of the Writing Skills of Accounting Majors in California" (unpublished study, 1987).
10. In a 2006 survey of its members in government conducted by the AICPA, 80% of respondents indicated written and oral communication skills were essential. See "AICPA Survey—Phase II: Government Members Foresee 'Brain Drain' in the Government Workforce," Government E-News, American Institute of Certified Public Accountants, 17 May 2006. http://fmcenter.aicpa.org/NR/rdonlyres/FA53AA12-25AF-4BCC-A25E-4281FCC56DBB/0/GPAC_NEWS_15.pdf (21 May 2007).
11. "Plain English Disclosure." Securities and Exchange Commission. *Staff Legal Bulletin No. 7(CF).* www.sec.gov/interps/legal/slbcf7.htm (9 April 2013): 1–2.
12. Marshall B. Romney and Paul J. Steinbart, *Accounting Information Systems*, 12th ed., © 2012, p. 53. Reprinted and Electronically reproduced by permission of Pearson Education, Inc., Upper Saddle River, New Jersey.
13. Duane R. Kullberg, William L. Gladstone, Peter R. Scanlon, J. Michael Cook, Ray J. Groves, Larry D. Horner, Shaun F. O'Malley, and Edward A. Kangas, *Perspectives on Education: Capabilities for Success in the Profession* (Big Eight Accounting Firms, 1989), 6.

The Writing Process: An Overview

Effective writing, like accounting, is a process. One step in the accounting process is to analyze transactions to determine how to record them. Several questions basic to the accounting system underlie your analysis of financial transactions and their treatment. What is the purpose of the information recorded and ultimately reported? Who are the users of this information, and what are their needs? Do the readers expect this information to be presented in a certain form, such as the typical presentations found in annual reports? How can the information be most fairly and effectively presented?

These questions are as important to good writing as they are to good accounting. Planning, which emphasizes both the purpose of the writing and the needs and expectations of the readers, is the first step in the writing process.

In this chapter, we discuss the writing process from beginning to end: planning for purpose and audience, including critical thinking about the issues; gathering information; generating and organizing ideas; drafting; revising; and proofreading. (Figure 1 summarizes the steps of the writing process.) You will learn how to apply this process to overcome much of the anxiety you may feel about writing, including the problem of writer's block. Throughout the chapter, we also discuss how computer technology can help you at every stage of the writing process.

You may become familiar with tips for effective writing that include content, critical thinking, appropriateness for readers, conciseness, clarity, coherence, and revision. In this chapter, discuss specific guidelines and techniques that will help you achieve these goals.

FIGURE 1 The Writing Process

Plan
- Read the assignment or consider the task carefully.
- Analyze the purposes of the document.
- Identify the accounting issues, including different ways those issues might be addressed.
- Analyze the issues from the readers' point of view. What are their interests, needs, and expectations?
- Gather and organize material.

Draft
- Write down your ideas.
- Don't stop to edit.
- Write the parts of the paper in whatever order you want.
- Keep your readers in mind as you compose.

Revise
- Reread the document from the readers' point of view. Is your treatment of the accounting issues fair, thorough, and persuasive?
- Revise the document so that it is clear, coherent, and concise.
- Proofread for grammatical, mechanical, and typographical errors.

GETTING STARTED: IDENTIFYING PURPOSE

One of the first stages in the writing process—analyzing the purpose of the document—is easy to overlook. When you think about purpose, you decide what you want to accomplish with your letter, memo, or other document. Do you want to provide your readers with information about some topic, answer their questions, recommend a course of action, persuade them to do something, or convince them to agree with you on some point?

These are just a few of the purposes a document can have. You should think carefully about the purpose *before* beginning to write. It might be helpful to think of your purpose in terms of three categories: to give information about something, to propose a course of action, or to solve a problem. The purpose of most writing tasks falls into one of these categories, or perhaps a combination of them.

As an example, assume you are the controller for Franklin Electrical Supplies. Franklin is considering purchasing stock in SolLite, Inc., one of Franklin's major suppliers of lighting fixtures. A report on this possible purchase could have any of the following purposes:

- To inform management of the advantages (or disadvantages) of the purchase
- To recommend that Franklin purchase (or not purchase) the stock
- To suggest a way to finance the purchase

The purpose of the report, or of any writing, determines what material it should contain. Consider another example. Your client, Coastal Development, is faced with a lawsuit that could result in a large loss. You might write a letter to Coastal's controller about the disclosure requirements for contingent loss liabilities as a result of pending litigation. In such a letter, you would not discuss gain contingencies or loss contingencies from bad debts. You would analyze the specific purpose of the letter to decide what information was relevant for this situation.

Another way to think about the purpose of a document is to identify the accounting issues it will address. Sometimes these issues are obvious, but at other times you must analyze the situation carefully before all the issues become apparent. For example, a client might seek your help on the best way to record a transaction to minimize income tax liability. As you analyze the transaction, you might become aware of accounting issues that would never occur to the client, such as the need to record the transaction consistently with generally accepted accounting principles (GAAP). You might also become aware of ethical or legal issues that the client had not considered.

Identifying the issues can help you define the purposes of the document you are writing, because one purpose might be to explain the accounting issues in a way your reader can understand.

After you have analyzed your purposes carefully, you should write them down. Be as specific as possible and try to define the purposes in a sentence. This sentence might later become part of the document's introduction.

When you analyze your purpose, *be specific*. Remember that you are writing to particular individuals in a particular situation. Relate the purpose of your writing to these people and their concerns. That is, state the purpose in the context of this specific situation rather than in broad, general terms. In the Franklin Electrical Supplies example, suppose you were writing a report on how to finance the purchase of SolLite, Inc., stock. You would limit your discussion to the financing alternatives available to Franklin that are practical for the company to consider.

Sometimes, to determine the purpose of a document, you need to read previous correspondence on the subject, such as a letter or email from a client. Be sure to read this correspondence carefully, noting important information and questions you've been asked to address. You may also receive an oral request to write something, perhaps from your supervisor. If you receive such a request to write, listen carefully to the directions. If the purpose of the document is not clear, ask questions until you're sure what the document should include.

THINKING CRITICALLY ABOUT THE ISSUES

If the purpose for your writing involves analyzing complex accounting issues, think carefully about your topic as you plan your document, gather information, and write. Sometimes the issues are complex: A problem might have more than one reasonable solution, and some people might disagree with the course of action you recommend. As you plan your writing, keep alternative points of view in mind. Consider not only the reasons for your own opinion, but also the reasons other people might have a different view. How will you support your opinion, and how will you respond to the arguments of people who disagree with you? Critical thinking about the issues throughout the writing process helps ensure that the document you write is persuasive. Your readers will regard you as knowledgeable and fair, and they will take seriously what you write.

ANALYZING THE READERS

When you are planning a writing task, it is important to consider who the readers will be. A memo on a highly technical accounting topic might be written one way for an accounting colleague, but another way for a client or manager with only limited knowledge of accounting procedures and terminology.

Effective writers analyze the needs and expectations of their readers before they begin to write. In writing a letter or memo, you will probably be writing to a limited number of people, perhaps to only one person. You also know, or can find out, important information about the reader or readers. Again, you must ask certain questions: How much do the readers know about the subject being discussed? What else do they need to know? Have they already formed opinions on the accounting issues? The answers to these questions, and perhaps others, will suggest the level at which you will write, including the terms and procedures you will explain, the background you will provide, and the arguments you will make.

Accountants who deal with the public should be particularly careful in analyzing the needs of their readers. A tax specialist, for example, might have clients with widely varying experience and knowledge of tax terminology. A corporate executive would probably understand such concepts as depreciation and accruals, but a small shopkeeper might not be familiar with this terminology. Business letters to these two clients, even on the same topic, should be written differently.

Consider the readers' attitudes and biases. Are your readers likely to be neutral to your recommendations, or will they need to be convinced? The critical thinking about the issues you have already done will help you write to your readers in a convincing way. Remember your readers' interests and concerns as you write. How will they benefit, directly or indirectly, from what you propose? How can you present your arguments to overcome their objections and biases? To answer this last question, you must anticipate readers' questions, research the issues, and then organize your arguments into a convincing sequence.

Other important considerations when analyzing your readers' needs and expectations are tone and style. What are their attitudes and biases? Some readers react well to an informal, friendly style of writing, but other readers believe that professional writing should be more formal. Whoever your readers are, remember always to be courteous. Whether you write in a technical or conversational style, all readers appreciate (and deserve) consideration, tact, and respect. Treating your readers with courtesy and respect will help ensure that your writing is ethical, as well as effective.

Word choices also contribute to an effective and responsible writing style. For example, many readers might find the following sentence troubling:

A successful *CEO* will treat *his* subordinates with respect.

Some readers might argue that the choice of pronouns (*CEO/his*) implies a gender bias. Use plural nouns and pronouns so that your language will be more inclusive:

Successful *CEOs* will treat *their* subordinates with respect.

Sometimes your readers will have additional expectations about your documents. In a classroom situation, the instructor usually gives directions about different aspects of your papers, such as format and due date. The instructor expects you to follow these directions. How well you do so usually affects your grade.

Readers' expectations are also important when you write on the job. Managers in some firms expect in-house memos and reports to follow certain conventions of format, organization, and style. If you work for such a firm, your memos and reports will seem more professional—and be more effective—if they are consistent with these expectations.

In fact, meeting readers' expectations might actually be a matter of company policy. Policies often govern how certain documents are written and what procedures they must go through for approval. Many professional services firms do not let new staff members send letters to clients unless a manager or partner first approves them. If you were a new staff member in such a firm, you might draft the client letter, but a manager or partner would review it and possibly ask you to make revisions. Moreover, for certain documents, such as some engagement letters and auditing reports, the actual language used in the letter might be determined by company policy. The partner will expect you to follow these policies with great care.

FIGURE 2 Planning a Paper

Consider these questions as you plan the documents you write:

1. Answer after you read and analyze the assignment or consider the task:
   - What are the accounting issues in this case?
   - Are there ethical issues I should consider?
   - What literature will I research to resolve these issues?
   - Who will read this document?
   - What different opinions might readers have about the issues?
   - What are the readers' concerns?
   - What are the purposes of this document?
2. Answer after you research and analyze the case:
   - What are the main points (conclusions) I need to make in this document?
   - What material should I include to make these conclusions clear and meaningful to the reader(s)?
   - How will I support my conclusions and respond to readers' objections?

In the example of the client letter just discussed, there are actually two or three readers: the manager and/or partner who reviews and approves the letter, and the client who receives it. This letter should be written on a technical level that is appropriate for the client, and it should address the client's concerns, but it should also meet the expectations of the manager and partner. Analyzing readers' needs, interests, and expectations is obviously more complex when there are several readers. Think carefully about the different readers and use your best judgment to meet the expectations of them all.

Analyzing readers' needs, expectations, and opinions is an important part of the preparation for writing. Planning, during which you think carefully about both your audience and your purpose, is the first guideline for effective writing. We'll add more to this list throughout the chapter.

1. **Analyze the purpose of the writing, the accounting issues involved, and the needs and expectations of the readers.**

Figure 2 summarizes questions you can ask yourself to help plan your writing.

GETTING YOUR IDEAS TOGETHER

After you have evaluated the purpose of the writing and the needs of the readers, you are ready for the second stage in the writing process: gathering information and organizing the ideas you want to present. This step might be quick and simple. For a short letter, you may not need to do further research; organizing your ideas may involve only a short list of the main topics you want to include in the letter—perhaps one topic for each paragraph.

For much of the writing you do, gathering information and organizing might be a more complicated process that involves much thought and perhaps some research as well. Let's look at some techniques you can use.

Gathering Information

Before you begin to write the document, be sure you have complete, accurate information. You can check the work that has already been done and then locate new information you'll need.

For many projects, some information might already be available. If you're working on an audit, for example, information might be available from other members of the audit team as well as from the files from the previous years' audits. Explore these sources of information fully. Review the files carefully and, when necessary, talk with the people who have already worked on the project.

Sometimes you might need to do additional research. This task can involve background reading on a technical topic or a careful review of professional standards or law, such as Financial Accounting Standards Board (FASB) publications, the tax code, IRS publications, or SEC publications. As you read this material, take notes carefully and be alert for information that might be helpful when you write. Remember also that accounting issues often have more than one possible solution. As you research, look for material that supports more than one point of view.

This research may require you to interview people who will be affected by the project that you are working on. Suppose you intend to propose in a report a new accounting information system for your company. You can gain important insights into topics your report should cover by talking with the people who would be affected by the proposed system. You can learn what they want the system to accomplish, what they might need to know about it, and whether they have already formed opinions that should be considered when you write your report.

Generating Ideas

After you have gathered the information you need, you are ready to begin the next phase of the writing process: deciding exactly what to say.

If you have not already written your statement of purpose, now is the time to do so. Try to break up the purpose into several subtopics. Suppose the purpose of a client letter is to recommend that the client company update its accounting system. The statement of purpose for this letter could specify the different accounting jobs for which the expanded system would be useful, outline its major advantages, and respond to questions and objections the client might have.

Another useful technique for generating ideas is brainstorming. With this technique, you think about your topic and write down all your ideas, in whatever order they come to you. Don't worry about organizing the ideas or evaluating them; later, you can consider how these ideas fit into the outline you developed when you analyzed the purposes of the document.

Brainstorming is often easier to do at the computer. As you type in the keywords and phrases that occur to you, the phrases might start to become sentences and the sentences might flow together to become paragraphs. You may find that the faster you record your ideas, the more freely the ideas flow. Thus, using a computer can be valuable when you need to generate ideas quickly.

Arranging Ideas: Organization

After you've decided what you want to say, it's important to consider how best to arrange these ideas so that the readers will find them easy to follow. In other words, it's time to think about how the document will be organized.

Much of the work you've already done will help you decide on the best pattern of organization. You may be able to use your statement of purpose as the basis of your organization, or your paper may be structured so that the readers' major concerns are your principle of organization—that is, each concern might be a major division of your paper. Some documents can be organized according to the accounting issues they address.

When considering all these approaches to organization, and possibly deciding among them, remember this principle: The needs and interests *of your readers* should determine the document's organization. Arrange your ideas in the order that they will find most helpful and easiest to follow. Anticipate when your readers are likely to raise objections or ask questions, and respond to those needs when they are likely to occur.

There are a few other points of organization to consider. First, most writing has the same basic structure: an introduction, a concise summary of important ideas, development of the main ideas, and a conclusion. This structure is shown in Figure 3. As you continue your studies, you will learn more about this basic structure as it is used for particular kinds of writing.

Another point is that ideas should be arranged in a logical order. To describe how to reconcile a bank statement, for instance, you would discuss each step of the procedure in the order in which it is performed.

Finally, you can often organize ideas according to their importance. In business writing, always arrange ideas from the most to the

FIGURE 3 Basic Writing Structure

- *Introduction:* identifies the subject of the document and tells why it was written. Sometimes the introduction also provides background information about the topic or stresses its importance. You may also use the introduction to build rapport with your reader, perhaps by mentioning a common interest or concern or referring to previous communication on the topic.
- *Concise statement of the main ideas:* summarizes explicitly main ideas, conclusions, or recommendations. This part of a document may be part of the introduction or a separate section. It can be as short as a one-sentence purpose statement or as long as a three-page executive summary.
- *Development of the main ideas:* Includes explanations, examples, analyses, steps, reasons, arguments, and factual details. This part of an outline or paper is often called the body.
- *Conclusion:* Brings the paper to an effective close. The conclusion may restate the main idea in a fresh way, suggest further work, or summarize recommendations, but an effective conclusion avoids unnecessary repetition.

least important. Note that this principle means you start with the ideas that are most important *to the reader.*

Suppose you are writing a report to recommend that your firm purchase new software for maintaining its accounting records. Naturally, you will want to emphasize the advantages of this purchase, describing them in the order that is likely to be most convincing to the readers. However, this investment might also have drawbacks, such as the problems involved in converting from the old system to the new one. For your report to appear well researched and unbiased, you need to include these disadvantages in your discussion. You might use the following structure:

I. Introduction, including your recommendation
II. Body
  A. Advantages, beginning with those most appealing to the readers
  B. Disadvantages, including, when possible, ways to minimize or overcome any drawbacks
III. Conclusion

One final word about organization: After you've decided how to arrange your ideas, it's a good idea to write an outline, if you haven't already done so. Having an outline in hand as you draft your paper will help you keep the paper on track. That way, you'll be sure to include all the information you had planned and avoid getting off the subject.

The guidelines for effective writing can now be expanded:

1. **Analyze the purpose of the writing, the accounting issues involved, and the needs and expectations of the readers.**
2. **Organize your ideas so that readers will find them easy to follow.**

WRITING THE DRAFT

The next major step in the writing process is writing the draft. The purpose of this step is to put your ideas in writing. Most writers find that they can write a first draft more easily if they don't try to edit at this stage. Spelling, punctuation, and style are thus not important in the draft. What is important is to write the ideas so that you can later polish and correct what you have written.

If you did your brainstorming at the computer, you may already have parts of your draft if the list of ideas you began with evolved into sentences or paragraphs as you typed.

The outline you have prepared will guide you as you write. However, you may decide to change the outline as you go, omitting some parts that no longer seem to fit or adding other ideas that seem necessary. Feel free to change the outline as you write; when you revise the draft later, you can make sure your thoughts are still well organized.

Although you will use your outline as a guide to the ideas you want to include in your draft, you might find it easier to write the various parts of the document in a different order from the one used in the outline. Some people find introductions hard to write, so they leave them until last. You may also choose to write the easiest sections of your draft first, or you may start writing some parts of the draft while you are still getting the material together for other parts.

One final word of advice on the draft stage: Don't allow yourself to get stuck while you search for the perfect word, phrase, or sentence. Leave a blank space, or write something that is more or less what you mean. You'll probably find the right words later.

REVISING THE DRAFT

The next stage in the writing process is the revision of the draft. In this step, you check your spelling and grammar, polish your style, and make a final check to see that the ideas are effectively and completely presented. As you revise, read the document *from the reader's point of view.*

You'll need to revise most of your writing more than once—perhaps three or four times. The key to revising is to let the writing get cold between revisions; a time lapse between readings enables you to read the draft more objectively and see what you have actually said, instead of what you meant to say. Ideally, revisions should be at least a day apart.

FIGURE 4 Examples of Homonyms

See (the verb)	sea (the body of water)
Bear (the animal)	bare (uncovered)
Deer (the animal)	dear (a term of address)
Plane (an airplane)	plain (unadorned)
Break (to divide into parts)	brake (to stop or slow)
Some (a certain amount)	sum (total)
Wood (made from trees)	would (the auxiliary verb)
Eye (what we see with)	I (the pronoun)
Threw (the verb)	through (the preposition)
Know (the verb)	no (negative)
Hour (time)	our (the pronoun)
Write (on paper or a computer)	right (correct)
Their (the pronoun)	there (place)
Which (the pronoun)	witch (the broom rider)
Site (location)	Cite (refer to a source)
Way (direction)	Weigh (determine weight)
So (therefore)	Sew (to stitch with thread)

Another technique is to have a colleague review the draft for both the content and the effectiveness of the writing. Choose a reviewer who is a good writer and evaluate the reviewer's suggestions with an open mind.

Most word processing software has the ability to check the text for grammar problems and certain errors in style, such as sentences that are too long and paragraphs that use the same word too often. The software may also identify some mistakes in punctuation, as well as most misspelled words.

A word of caution about these style analyzers, spell checkers, and grammar checkers—they're not infallible. They can't catch all the weaknesses in your text, and sometimes they flag problems that aren't really there. If you use a computer to analyze your writing, you still must use your own judgment about what changes to make.

Homonyms can cause problems with your writing, for example, but spell checkers and grammar checkers may not find this kind of problem. Homonyms are words that sound the same when spoken aloud, but they have different spellings and meanings. Figure 4 shows examples of homonyms that spell checkers or grammar checkers may not recognize.

Another revision technique is to print the document and edit the hard copy by hand. You can then make the revisions in your computer file later. Some writers find that they revise more effectively if they work with a hard copy rather than text on a screen.

As you continue your study of writing, you will learn more about what to look for when putting your written work in final form.

We now have three guidelines for effective writing:

1. **Analyze the purpose of the writing, the accounting issues involved, and the needs and expectations of the readers.**
2. **Organize your ideas so that readers will find them easy to follow.**
3. **Write the draft and then revise it to make the writing polished and correct.**

THE FINAL DRAFT

After you have polished the style and organization of the paper, you will be ready to put it in final form. Consider questions of document design, such as the use of headings, white space, and other elements of the paper's appearance.

Proofreading is also an important step. Here are some suggestions for effective proofreading:

1. Proofreading is usually more effective if you leave time between typing and looking for errors. You will be able to critique the paper more clearly if you have been away from it for a while.
2. Use your computer's spell check program to eliminate spelling and typographical errors. Remember that the computer program cannot distinguish between homonyms such as *their* and *there* or *affect* and *effect*.
3. In addition to your computer's spell checker, you may also need to use a dictionary to look up any word that could possibly be misspelled, such as words the computer doesn't recognize, or homonyms it may not have flagged. Check also that you've spelled people's names correctly. If you are a poor speller, have someone else read the paper for spelling errors.
4. If you know that you tend to make a certain type of error, read through your paper at least once to check for that error. For example, if you have problems with subject-verb agreement, check every sentence in your paper to be sure the verbs are correct.
5. Read your paper *backwards*, sentence by sentence, as a final proofreading step. This technique isolates each sentence and makes it easier to spot errors you may have overlooked in previous readings.

DEALING WITH WRITER'S BLOCK

Writer's block is a problem everyone faces at some time or another. We stare at blank paper or at a blank screen with no idea of how to get started. The ideas and the words just don't come.

Many of the techniques already discussed in this chapter will help you overcome writer's block. Thinking of writing as a process, rather than a completed product that appears suddenly in its final form, should help make the job less formidable. Any difficult task seems easier if you break it down into manageable steps.

The discussions of the steps in the writing process, especially the section on writing the draft, included suggestions that will help you overcome writer's block. Here is a summary of these techniques:

1. Plan before you write so that you know what you need to say.
2. Write with an outline in view, but write the paper in any order you want. You can rearrange it later.
3. Don't strive for perfection in the draft stage. Leave problems of grammar, spelling, style, and so forth to the revision stage.
4. Begin with the easiest sections to write.
5. Don't get stuck on difficult places. Skip over them and go on to something else. You may find that when you come back to the rough spots later, they are not as hard to write as you thought.

WRITING UNDER PRESSURE

Throughout this chapter, you've seen how writing is easier if you break the project down into steps. It's easy to manage these steps when you have plenty of time to plan, research, draft, revise, and polish.

What about situations in which you don't have the luxury of time? What about writing essay questions on an exam, or on-the-job writing tasks where you have only a little while to produce a letter or memo?

The truth is that any writing project, no matter how hurriedly it must be done, will go more smoothly if you stick with the three basic steps of the writing process: plan, draft, and revise. Even if you have only a few minutes to work on a document, allow yourself some of that time to think about whom you're writing to, what you need to say, and the best way to organize that material. Then draft the paper.

Allow yourself some time to revise as well. Use a spell check program to help locate embarrassing spelling and typographical errors.

WRITING AND ELECTRONIC MEDIA

Some of the writing you will do as a professional accountant will be for electronic transmission, such as email or other documents that are sent over the Internet. Documents sent electronically should be planned, written, and revised with the same care you would use for hard-copy versions. This may be obvious for formal documents, but even email and instant messaging (IM), which we often send in haste and consider to be extremely informal, requires care in order to be effective.

HELP FROM COLLEAGUES: CRITIQUING

Once you have improved your document as much as you can, you may have another source of help: constructive feedback from one or more colleagues. If you are preparing an assignment for a course, this help may come from other students in the class. In a job situation, you might ask a colleague to review your writing. You will, of course, be willing to return the favor to your colleagues if they ask you to critique their writing.

Here are some tips for giving helpful critiques:

- Reviews of the writing should be both tactful and honest.
- Always point out strengths of the writing, and then make a few suggestions if you see ways the writing could be improved.
- Make suggestions in positive ways, and be as specific as possible. For example, you wouldn't say, "I can't make any sense of this, and your grammar is deplorable!" Rather, you might say, "Can you explain this concept more clearly? Perhaps shorter sentences would help. Also, you might want to check your verbs."
- Ask the writer if you can write your feedback on the paper itself. Then be prepared to discuss what you liked about the paper, as well as ways it could be improved.

If a colleague critiques your writing, here are some things to keep in mind:

- Whenever possible, ask people to critique your writing who are themselves good writers.
- Keep an open mind, and resist the natural temptation to be defensive. On the other hand, remember that final responsibility for the document is yours; you'll decide which suggestions to use. Not all advice, however well intended, is helpful.
- Thank the reviewers for their help.

EXERCISES

Exercise 1 [General]

Analyze the letter in Figure 5. How would you react if you received this letter?

1. Think about these questions and then discuss them with your classmates:
   - What are the strengths of this letter? (It does have some strengths!)
   - What are the weaknesses of the letter? (Hint: Can you find all the typos and spelling errors? In addition to these problems,

FIGURE 5 Letter for Exercise 1: What Is Wrong with This Letter?

Wright and Wrongh, CPAs
123 Anystreet
Anytown, US 12345

Corner Dress Shop
123 Anyother Street
Anytown, US 12345

Gentleman

We are in receipt of your correspondence and beg to thank you.

After extensive research we have found what we hope will be a satisfactory responce to your questions, we hope you will find our work satisfactory. It is the goal of our firm to alway offer the best, most expert and reliable service possible to all our clients, all of whom are value and with whom we hope to have a lont-term working relationship to our mutual advantage.

There were two possibilities for the resolution of this issue that we considered after a careful analyses of the applicable IRC sections to your situation. If the first possibility proved relevant, then you would be subject to a fine of $5500, plus penalties and interest. If athe other possibility was the best solution, then you would receive a $4400 credit because of a loss carryforard to your current year returns. As you no doubt know, IRC Sec.341(6)a [paras. 5-9] stipulate that the regulations we must follow. Thus, to be in compliance with the rules and regs. you must follow the provisions of the pertinent sections.

As your CPAs, we are most concerned that we be in complianse with all standards of professional ethics, and we always keep this in mind when we advise you on your tax and accounting questions. We don't want to go to jail, and we're sure you don't either!

After extensive research, we advise you to file an amended return immediately because the first possibility enumerated in the above paragraph proves to be the correct solution to your problem.

Thanking you in advance, we remain

Yours with highest regards,

M. Ostley Wrongh

M. Ostley Wrongh
Wright and Wrongh, CPAs

the letter has a number of less obvious weaknesses. What are they?)

2. Revise the letter so that it is more effective. Invent any details you may need.

Exercise 2 [General]

You are a member of Beta Alpha Psi (the accounting honorary society) at a major university. A large local high school has contacted your chapter of the honorary society and asked it to prepare a two-page flyer about opportunities provided by an accounting career and the skills (hard and soft) required to succeed both as an accounting student and as an accounting professional. You have been asked by the president of the honorary society, Sandy West, to write the flyer. She has asked that you prepare it in the form of a memo written to her. Write a memo to Sandy West responding to her request.

Exercise 3 [Managerial]

Jim Kakes, CEO of Kakes Manufacturing Company, needs to hire a new controller as the current controller is retiring. Several other CEOs he knows have suggested he look for someone who is a Certified Management Accountant (CMA). Mr. Kakes is not familiar with this designation and has asked you what it is and whether you believe hiring a CMA would be a good idea, given the extra amount he will have to pay in salary,

Write a memo to Mr. Kakes responding to his request.

Exercise 4 [Systems]

You are employed by the consulting division of a large professional services firm. Your expertise is in information systems auditing. You have become interested in gaining professional certification in this area and are aware of an organization, ISACA (formerly known as the Information Systems Audit and Control Association and now known by its acronym only) which offers certification as a CISA (Certified Information Systems Auditor). Write a memo to the head of the consulting division, Mr. Robert Sherrill, requesting that your firm provide the funds for you to attain this certification. You should, of course, explain what this credential is and the benefits to your firm of having a CISA on staff. You have researched the possibility and believe you will need approximately $1,100 to cover the expenses of preparing for and taking the CISA exam.

Exercise 5 [Managerial/Current Professional Issues]

In 2012, The American Institute of Certified Public Accountants (AICPA) and the Chartered Institute of Management Accountants

(CIMA) entered into a joint venture to offer a new credential, the Chartered Global Management Accountant (CGMA). Write an article for your school's accounting club newsletter discussing this new credential, what its advantages are, and how to obtain it.

Exercise 6 [Auditing]

You are a partner in a medium-size CPA firm and want to convince your partners that the firm should expand the services provided to clients. Specifically, you believe the firm should begin offering *WebTrust* and *SysTrust* services.

Write a memo to your partners to explain what the concepts of *WebTrust* and *SysTrust* services are and why your firm should begin to offer such services.

Exercise 7 [Tax]

Your school's accounting honorary society maintains a Web site on which it includes short articles on various accounting topics. The readers of this Web site are primarily other accounting students. The Web master has asked you to write a short article explaining the differences among progressive, proportional, and regressive tax systems, including their relative advantages and disadvantages. Give examples.

Exercise 8 [Financial]

For decades, there has been a debate as to whether different GAAP should be established for private companies as opposed to public companies. Often, this has been referred to as the "Big GAAP vs. Little GAAP" controversy. In mid-2012, the Financial Accounting Foundation's board of trustees voted to establish a Private Company Council to determine whether exceptions or modifications to GAAP for privately held companies should be made.

Prepare an outline you can use for a speech to your accounting club on the pros and cons of modifying GAAP for privately held companies.

Exercise 9 [International]

For many years, the IFRS (International Financial Reporting Standards) Foundation has worked to develop and promote the adoption of a single set of International Financial Reporting Standards (IFRSs) that are globally accepted. It has done this through its standard-setting body, the International Accounting Standards Board (IASB).

An article in *Accounting Today* entitled "IFRS Foundation Charts IFRS Progress" (http://www.accountingtoday.com/news/IFRS-Foundation-Charts-IFRS-Progress-67016-1.html) reported on the first phase of a study by the IFRS Foundation on progress toward global adoption of IFRSs.

Prepare an outline you can use for a speech to your accounting club on the pros and cons of global adoption of IFRSs, the progress made toward global adoption, and prospects for completion of the effort by the IFRS Foundation.

Critical Thinking

Critical thinking skills are important to the analysis and communication of accounting information. *Critical thinking* can be defined as fair, open-minded thinking that asks appropriate questions and considers all relevant information before reaching a conclusion. Critical thinkers consider problems from multiple points of view before reaching a decision, and they are careful to avoid errors in reasoning, which are called logical fallacies. They also use precise, clear language to construct unambiguous arguments that readers can understand and, in turn, evaluate fairly. In other words, critical thinkers analyze issues and communicate information responsibly; critical thinking is thus a component of ethical responsibility. And critical thinking is inseparable from effective communication.

The AICPA recognizes the importance of critical thinking and evaluates those skills on the CPA exam. In its "Content and Skill Specifications for the Uniform CPA Examination," the AICPA specifies "Complex Problem Solving and Judgment."[1] Included in this skill set are these elements of critical thinking:

- Apply professional skepticism, which is an attitude that includes a questioning mind and a critical assessment of information or evidence obtained.
- Identify and solve unstructured problems.
- Develop reasonable hypotheses to answer a question or resolve a problem.
- Formulate and examine alternative solutions in terms of their relative strengths and weaknesses, level of risk, and appropriateness for a given situation.
- Develop logical conclusions through the use of inductive and deductive reasoning.

As you will see, this chapter illustrates how you can develop these and other critical thinking skills. We will discuss the process of

From Chapter 7 of *Effective Writing: A Handbook for Accountants,* Tenth Edition. Claire B. May, Gordon S. May.

constructing an argument, two approaches to logical reasoning, and some of the fallacies you should recognize and avoid. We will then show how you can use critical thinking to resolve ethical dilemmas.

MAKING AN ARGUMENT: THE PROCESS

As a practicing professional, you will sometimes be asked to recommend a course of action for your firm or for your clients. To derive a sound recommendation, you must construct an argument. This process can be divided into six steps:

1. Identify the key issues.
2. Anticipate all sides to an argument.
3. Research all sides to the argument, using authoritative sources.
4. Weigh the evidence for all sides to the argument, and build support for your position.
5. Identify and respond to counterarguments.
6. Communicate your conclusions.

To illustrate the process, consider this hypothetical scenario. You are an accountant employed by a medium-size accounting firm. The firm has twenty accountants on its staff, in addition to technical and clerical support staff. The firm has had its offices in a grand old office building in the downtown heart of the city for the past sixty years. However, the owners of the building have decided to convert the building to residential condominiums, forcing your firm to relocate. You have been asked to recommend the best alternative for the new office. After researching the alternatives, you will present your recommendation in a memo to the firm's partners. How do you form and communicate your recommendation? The process listed previously will help you as you construct an argument to support your conclusions.

A word of caution is in order here: Remember that it's always important to consider the expectations of your readers and the purpose of the document you are writing. What are the expectations of the partners who asked you to investigate the relocation problem? Do they expect you to identify the one best site for the firm, or have they asked you to recommend several viable locations, giving the advantages and disadvantages of each choice? In the latter case, the partners themselves would make the final selection, based on the information you have provided. You would have narrowed the field, then, through your analysis and research. For the purposes of this hypothetical example, assume that the partners have asked you to recommend what you have identified as the best site. They will expect you to document the thoroughness with which you investigated the alternatives and the reasons for your conclusions.

1. *Identify key issues.* The first step in constructing an argument is to identify the key issues. In the situation just described, the most important issues might be, first, where in the city the new office should be located, and second, whether the firm should lease office space, purchase an office condominium, purchase its own building, or construct its own building. Each of these major issues should be further analyzed. You should consider the availability and costs of suitable space, the suitability of potential sites for the firm's business, and the accounting implications of the decision to lease, purchase, or construct.
2. *Anticipate all sides to the argument.* Before you reach your conclusions, you need to identify all the reasonable alternatives. With preliminary research, you'll gather information about the obvious choices. You also need to identify the preferences of other people involved in the decision and take account of their knowledge, experience, assumptions, and biases. It's especially important to consider the views of those who will make the final decision, in this case the firm's partners. Listen carefully to what other people say, read carefully what they have written on the issues in question, and, where appropriate, ask them to clarify their views or make preliminary suggestions for the best solution to the problem. For example, before you suggest leasing, purchasing, or constructing in this scenario, find out if the partners are willing to consider all three possibilities. You should also determine which sections of the city they believe to be viable locations for the firm. Are they determined to maintain the firm's office in the center of the city, or would they consider moving to a midtown or suburban location?
3. *Research all sides to the argument, using authoritative sources.* After you have identified the alternative solutions to your problem, you can research the possibilities, including sources for both accounting and non-accounting information. Consider your firm's needs and how alternative sites would accommodate those needs. Is the location convenient to the firm's employees and clients, and is the location suitable for business? Is adequate parking and/or public transportation available for the firm's employees and clients? What other businesses are located in this area? Would proposed buildings require renovation? What are the costs, in both time and money, of these renovations, as well as other moving costs? All these decisions involve accounting considerations, which you also must research. What are the accounting and tax implications of the decision to lease, purchase, or construct? Refer to specific GAAP and tax provisions for these scenarios.
4. *Weigh the evidence for all sides to the argument, and build support for your position.* After you've analyzed the information you find in your research, the solution may be obvious. In this example,

assume that you have identified the best site for the firm's relocation after weighing the pros and cons of all alternatives, and that you are ready to give the reasons for your conclusions. Building support for your conclusions involves organizing your ideas and materials in a logical order. This organization might take the form of an outline: the key issues, the recommendations, and the reasons to support your recommendations, from most to least important.

5. *Identify and respond to counterarguments.* In this office relocation example, some of the partners may have initial preferences for a particular location, or they may raise objections to the site you've selected. You should identify in advance the reasons why some of the partners might disagree with your conclusions. That is, you must identify the counterarguments (arguments against your recommendations). You must also decide how you will respond to these objections—whether you will agree with them (concede the counterarguments) or argue against them (refute the counterarguments).

   The response to a counterargument may be a combination of concession and refutation. For instance, one of the partners in this example may object to your recommendations because the site you've chosen requires extensive, costly renovation. You might concede that those costs will be high, but also point out that over time the costs will be more than made up because the cost of the new lease (or purchase) will be considerably lower than the cost of the firm's current lease.

   Sometimes people constructing an argument believe that presenting all sides of the argument will weaken their position. Just the opposite is the case, however. By presenting all sides, you'll create the impression that you are a responsible person who has carefully considered all sides of an issue before reaching a conclusion. Thus, people will find you credible and fair, and they will take your argument seriously.

   To complete this step successfully, keep an open mind and imagine the situation from multiple points of view. Review the questions you asked in step 2 or ask additional questions. In our example, it might even be appropriate for you to seek preliminary feedback on your conclusions from your partners, before you present your final recommendation.

6. *Communicate your conclusions.* In this step, you present your conclusions and your reasons, along with the counterarguments to your recommendations that you have anticipated and your response to those counterarguments. You may present your conclusions orally, perhaps in a meeting, or in a written document such as a memo, letter, or report. In this example, you'll write a memo as the partners have requested. For a written document, you should apply all of the effective writing techniques you have learned. You may,

of course, be asked to present your recommendations in both oral and written formats.

Reaching Sound Conclusions: Two Approaches to Logic

Critical thinking is the construction of an argument, often in a manner such as the process just outlined. It may also be thought of as an exercise of logic, which is defined as the practice of good reasoning. The science of logic is often divided into inductive and deductive reasoning. The ability to use inductive and deductive reasoning is among the skills tested on the CPA exam. In this chapter, we discuss these forms of reasoning further, as well as some of the more commonly made errors in reasoning, which are called fallacies.

Inductive Reasoning

The process used to construct an argument in the office relocation scenario discussed earlier demonstrates one form of inductive reasoning: gathering evidence, and then reaching a conclusion. More formally, inductive reasoning is defined as reaching conclusions about the entirety of something (the whole) from a study of representative examples (parts of that whole). The scientific method of research is one example of inductive reasoning: observing samples, gathering data, and drawing tentative conclusions, or hypotheses, which are then further tested for verification. Some variations of inductive reasoning include making comparisons (drawing analogies), analyzing causes, conducting surveys, referring to authoritative sources, and citing statistics. In short, inductive reasoning begins with specific facts and from these facts derives general conclusions or principles.

Deductive Reasoning

With inductive reasoning, you gather specific information and then reach a general conclusion. With deductive reasoning, you apply reasoning in the opposite direction; you begin with one or more general assumptions or premises and arrive at a specific conclusion. Consider these examples:

> All accounting majors at this university must take a course in tax accounting.
>
> Jenny is an accounting major at this university.
>
> Therefore, Jenny must take a course in tax accounting.

Deductive reasoning is often stated in the form of a syllogism. A *syllogism* consists of a major premise, a minor premise, and a conclusion. In the preceding example, the first line is the major premise, the second line is the minor premise, and the third line is the conclusion.

Here's another example of a syllogism:

MAJOR PREMISE: Asset account balances increase with debits.
MINOR PREMISE: The asset account was debited.
CONCLUSION: The asset account balance increased.

To reach sound conclusions using deductive reasoning, you must be sure your arguments are both valid and sound. These terms—*valid* and *sound*—will become clearer with examples. First, a valid argument is one in which the conclusion has been correctly drawn from the premises. Study the following examples:

Example 1: Valid argument:

MAJOR PREMISE: All the students in this class have passed the placement test.
MINOR PREMISE: Robert is a student in this class.
CONCLUSION: Therefore, Robert has passed the placement test.

Example 2: Invalid argument:

MAJOR PREMISE: All the students in this class have passed the placement test.
MINOR PREMISE: Robert has passed the placement test.
CONCLUSION: Therefore, Robert is a student in this class.

In the valid argument in Example 1, the conclusion has been correctly drawn from the premises, unlike the invalid argument in Example 2. In Example 2, even though Robert has passed the placement test, he might not be a student in the class for any number of reasons. He might have taken the class in an earlier semester, postponed the class until a later semester, be enrolled in a different section of the class, changed his major, or transferred to another school.

Let's look at two more examples. Example 3 is a valid argument—the conclusion has been correctly drawn from the premises—but Example 4 is invalid:

Example 3: Valid argument:

MAJOR PREMISE: All publicly held companies must construct financial statements following GAAP.
MINOR PREMISE: Brite Company is a publicly held company
CONCLUSION: Therefore, Brite Company must construct its financial statements following GAAP.

Example 4: Invalid argument:

MAJOR PREMISE: All publicly held companies must construct financial statements following GAAP.
MINOR PREMISE: Brite Company constructs its financial statements following GAAP.
CONCLUSION: Brite Company is a publicly held company.

Many companies that are not publicly held also construct financial statements following GAAP. Thus, Brite Company might not be publicly held.

Deductive reasoning must be *sound*, as well as valid, for the conclusions to be true. Sound reasoning requires not only (a) that the conclusion has been correctly drawn from the premises, but also (b) that the premises are themselves true. For a sound conclusion, both the major and minor premises must be true. For instance, in the preceding Example 1, the conclusion would not be sound if either the major or minor premise is not true: (1) some students in the class have not passed the placement test, or (2) Robert is not a student in the class.

Sometimes the use of a syllogism will help you spot errors in reasoning. Consider the following example:

> The SEC has filed charges against The Gigantic National Corporation for cheating its former employees out of their pension benefits. Larry Womack, the CEO, issues this statement to the press: "The buck stops here. As CEO, I must accept responsibility for the fraud uncovered by the SEC. A few unscrupulous middle managers have violated company policy and the law by authorizing and carrying out this fraud. Those responsible will be identified, and will no longer work for this corporation. I deplore what has happened, but I will not resign."

What is wrong with the reasoning expressed in Mr. Womack's statement? We can analyze his argument in the form of a syllogism such as this one:

MAJOR PREMISE:	The person(s) responsible for the fraud will no longer work for this corporation.
MINOR PREMISE:	I am responsible for the fraud. (Recall the CEO's assertion: "I must accept responsibility for the fraud uncovered by the SEC.")
CONCLUSION:	I will not resign.

You can see that the conclusion in this case does not follow logically from the major and minor premises. This argument is invalid. Put another way, the CEO has contradicted himself.

Fallacies: Mistakes in Reasoning

To reach sound conclusions, you must be careful to avoid mistakes in reasoning. That is, you must learn to recognize and avoid fallacies in the arguments you make or those made by others. We have already considered the requirements that a deductive argument be both valid and sound; that is, the argument must avoid the fallacies of drawing improper conclusions from the premises, or reasoning from false premises. Some other common fallacies that you should also avoid are listed here along with examples of each:

- ***Fallacies involving language:*** Using ambiguous word choices (vague or undefined), loaded language, labels, and slogans

  Anyone who favors the passage of this legislation is unpatriotic.

  (What does *unpatriotic* mean in this case? This word, as it is used here, is vague and loaded. That is, it may generate an emotional response unrelated to critical thinking about the legislation in question.)

- ***Fallacies involving appeals to emotion:*** Appealing to fear, pity, anger, or prejudice

  If we change our pension plan, widows and orphans will suffer.

  (This argument illustrates an appeal to pity. Of course, decision makers should consider the effects of the proposed change on pension recipients, but other factors should also be evaluated. It might be, for example, that the company will go bankrupt if it doesn't change its pension plan.)

- ***Fallacy of appeal to tradition:*** Arguing for something only because it's customary

  We shouldn't promote Joanne Risling to a partner position. Her degree is from a private university. It's tradition that our partners graduate from the state university.

- ***Fallacy of false authority:*** Using authorities that are unidentified, irrelevant, or lacking proper credentials

  Experts agree that all accounting firms should be involved in social media.

  (Who are these experts?)

  We should invest in this stock, because all our friends are buying it.

  (This statement illustrates a type of false authority called the bandwagon fallacy: "Get on the bandwagon and do what everybody else is doing.")

- ***Ad hominem fallacy:*** Attacking opponents' character, rather than their arguments

  Don't listen to what he's saying. He's an idiot.

- ***Post hoc fallacy:*** Assuming that because one circumstance happens before another, the first circumstance is the cause of the second

  After we hired Stan Sterling, our company's profits increased. Clearly Stan is the reason for our increased profitability.

  (Hiring Stan may indeed have affected the company's profits; however, we need more information before reaching this conclusion. What is Stan's position? What other factors, such as changes in the market, might be responsible for the growth in profits?)

- ***Hasty generalization fallacy:*** Using poor or inadequate sampling techniques

Professor Brown is a poor teacher. I know this because my roommate took his tax accounting course and complained about it every day.

Clearly, Jan Smith will be elected class president. I asked three of the people on my hall, and all of them plan to vote for Smith.

- ***Either/or fallacy (false dilemma):*** Assuming there are only two choices, when there may be several

  You're either for me or against me.

  (I may support you as a general rule, but disagree with you on this particular point.)

  Either we adopt this measure, or we face bankruptcy.

  (We might adopt a different measure and avoid bankruptcy.)

- ***Slippery slope fallacy*** Arguing that if one event occurs, a series of undesirable events will inevitably occur as a result

  If we provide cell phones to our sales staff, the next thing you know they'll demand their own laptop computers, then company cars, and then chauffeurs to drive those cars. They'll then want unlimited expense accounts for trips to Las Vegas. The company will go bankrupt.

Earlier, we defined critical thinking as fair, open-minded thinking that asks appropriate questions and considers all relevant information before reaching a conclusion. Although there is no formula for achieving critical thinking, if you keep in mind the factors we have discussed in this chapter, your thinking will be much more responsible, enabling you to be a more effective communicator.

Critical Thinking and Ethical Dilemmas

Ethics is important in the practice of accounting. Accountants are expected to uphold a high standard of ethics in the practice of their professional responsibilities. They find guidance for making ethical decisions in legal requirements, codes of ethics (such as the AICPA's Code of Professional Ethics or the IMA's Statement of Ethical Professional Practice), and their personal ethical values. Often what constitutes ethical behavior is obvious, but sometimes accountants face complex situations for which the ethical solution is not immediately clear. Critical thinking can help resolve these ethical dilemmas.

The process for resolving ethical dilemmas resembles the steps you take to make a strong argument, as discussed earlier in this chapter. Indeed, identifying and defending a course of action as the most ethical among several alternatives is itself a kind of argument, even if one you have only with yourself. When you are faced with a situation that requires you to make an ethical decision, follow these steps:

1. Obtain all the facts relevant to the situation.
2. Identify all the ethical issues.
3. Determine who will be affected by the way these issues are resolved. Consider both individuals and groups, such as shareholders, employees, and the general public.
4. Identify alternative solutions to the issues, including arguments that might be used to support each alternative.
5. Analyze how the individuals and groups identified in step 3 would be affected by the alternative solutions.
6. Consider guidelines for ethical decisions, such as applicable legal requirements, codes of ethics, and your own ethical values. Be careful to avoid logical fallacies in your thinking.
7. Decide on the appropriate action and, when necessary, communicate your decision to the appropriate parties. If the situation is potentially contentious, be prepared to provide the reasons for your decision. When you write or speak to someone about the ethical issues, be especially tactful, courteous, and respectful to all parties concerned.

As you can see, resolving ethical dilemmas depends on critical thinking, as well as effective communication.

EXERCISES

Exercise 1 [General]

The following statements contain mistakes in reasoning (fallacies). Which fallacies are illustrated here? (Some statements may illustrate more than one fallacy.)

1. Ever since she changed accountants, the profits in her business have increased. Clearly the new accountant knows how to cook the books.
2. Give them an inch and they'll take a mile.
3. Either we redesign all our accounting information systems or we might as well close down the business.
4. Don't listen to him. He's just a nerdy, detail-obsessed accountant.
5. Three out of four accountants agree: *The Daily Balance Sheet* is the best source of financial news.
6. We don't need more public transportation in our city. Everyone in my office agrees they'd rather drive their own cars.
7. We've used Biddy and Bully as our firm's legal firm for four generations. Even though their work has become unsatisfactory, I wouldn't want to change firms.
8. We shouldn't hire Jim Blankenship. He's from Hick City, and everybody knows people from there are just a bunch of ignorant buffoons.

Exercise 2 [Ethics]

You are a partner in a medium-size CPA firm. One of your clients, Paul Garcia, who owns PG Corporation, has indicated a desire to report higher net income for his business this year because the company plans to apply for a loan at the bank. In an effort to increase reported net income, Mr. Garcia has told his accounting department to book immediately some large sales for which contracts have been signed but for which the goods will not be manufactured or shipped until after the first of the year. Write a letter to Mr. Gracia concerning your position on this issue.

Exercise 3 [General]

Your school is considering a new attendance policy. If this policy is adopted, students will be allowed only three absences for each class during the term. After the fourth absence, the registrar's office will suspend the student. Suspended students will be allowed to appeal the suspension if they can offer documented evidence that they missed the classes for legitimate reasons, such as illness, a death in the family, or jury duty.

Do you believe the new attendance policy should be adopted? Following the guidelines for critical thinking discussed in this chapter, decide where you stand on this issue. (Remember the importance of identifying and responding to counterarguments.) After you have formed your conclusions, write your argument in the form of a letter to the Dean of Students at your school.

Exercise 4 [General]

Some administrators in your school have proposed a change in grading policy for major level courses—that is, beyond the principles or introductory level. They propose that instructors be required to grade courses on a Pass/Fail basis only. What would be the advantages and disadvantages of this proposed policy? Consider both sides of this question, using critical thinking to analyze the pros and cons of the proposal. Then write a letter to the editor of your school's newspaper, or the local newspaper where your school is located, in which you summarize your findings.

Exercise 5 [Financial/Ethics]

You are a staff accountant at Outrageous Corporation. The controller of the company, Howard Eino, is concerned that profits reported in the annual report will not meet those forecast at the beginning of the year. He has asked you to decrease the amount of annual depreciation charged on certain equipment by revising the estimated life. When you tell Mr. Eino that revision of useful life solely to "manage" profit is not appropriate, he responds by saying, "Oh, everybody does it." You realize that if you fail to do what your boss wants, you may receive an unfavorable annual performance evaluation. How will you resolve this dilemma?

To help yourself think through this problem, you've decided to write an outline in which you'll record the issues, relevant information, your reasoning, and the course of action you finally decide to take. You won't show the outline to anyone else, but you want it to be complete and well-organized, so that your thinking will be clear. Write the outline.

Exercise 6 [General]

Look for illustrations of the fallacies discussed in this chapter in print media, on radio or television, on the Internet, or in the conversations you hear. Quote or paraphrase the passage that illustrates the fallacy, giving a citation of the source. Then identify the fallacy and explain the error in reasoning the passage demonstrates.

Exercise 7 [Financial/Theory]

Some people would argue that historical costs should no longer be used in accounting because they are not relevant. Others argue that departing from historical cost introduces too much subjectivity into accounting. Write out a detailed outline for a presentation to your class providing a defense of both points of view and then explain why the FASB has chosen to depart from historical cost in many of its accounting standards.

Exercise 8 [Auditing/Theory]

Some have suggested eliminating the provision of Rule 203 of the AICPA's professional ethics that permits non-conformance with GAAP if, in the opinion of the CPA, following GAAP would result in misleading financial statements. Thoroughly discuss the pros and cons of eliminating this provision of Rule 203 and present a convincing argument as to whether it should or should not be eliminated.

Prepare your argument in the form of a memo to the managing partner of your CPA firm, Elaine Morgan.

Exercise 9 [Financial/International/Current Professional Issues]

In 2010, the International Accounting Standards Board (IASB) changed its constitution to emphasize the adoption of International Financial Reporting Standards (IFRSs), rather than simply convergence of those standards with standards issued by individual countries. Write an essay on whether the SEC should support convergence between United States GAAP and IFRSs, or whether the SEC should support adoption of IFRSs. Your essay should demonstrate your understanding of critical thinking. Assume the audience for your essay is accounting students in your class.

Exercise 10 [Tax]

Write an essay that addresses the purpose, structure, and recent activities of the IRS Oversight Board. Include a discussion of its strategy to reduce the "tax gap," that is, to reduce the amount of uncollected taxes. Your essay should demonstrate your understanding of critical thinking. Assume the audience for your essay is accounting students in your class.

Exercise 11 [Systems]

Write a brief article for your accounting honorary society's Web page about the kinds of issues that must be considered when designing an accounting information system. Your purpose is to generate interest among the students in taking an accounting information systems course.

Exercise 12 [Managerial]

Your accounting honorary society's Web page is running a series of articles about various careers in accounting that accounting students might choose. You have been asked to write an article about the advantages of a career in management accounting. Write the article with the purpose of persuading students to seek a career in management accounting without discouraging them from considering other career choices.

NOTE

1. American Institute of Certified Public Accountants (AICPA), *Content and Skill Specifications for the Uniform CPA Examination,* Update Approved October 1, 2011, Effective Date January 1, 2013. (New York: AICPA), 37–38.

Introduction to Corporate Governance

Corporate governance has become a well-discussed and controversial topic in both the popular and business press. Newspapers produce detailed accounts of corporate fraud, accounting scandals, insider trading, excessive compensation, and other perceived organizational failures—many of which culminate in lawsuits, resignations, and bankruptcy. The stories have run the gamut from the shocking and instructive (epitomized by Enron and the elaborate use of special-purpose entities and aggressive accounting to distort its financial condition) to the shocking and outrageous (epitomized by Tyco partially funding a $2.1 million birthday party in 2002 for the wife of Chief Executive Officer [CEO] Dennis Kozlowski that included a vodka-dispensing replica of the statue *David*). Central to these stories is the assumption that somehow *corporate governance* is to blame—that is, the system of checks and balances meant to prevent abuse by executives failed (see the following sidebar).[1]

A Breakdown in Corporate Governance: HealthSouth

Consider HealthSouth Corp., the once high-flying healthcare service provider based in Birmingham, Alabama.[2]

- CEO Richard Scrushy and other corporate officers were accused of overstating earnings by at least $1.4 billion between 1999 and 2002 to meet analyst expectations.[3]
- The CEO was paid a salary of $4.0 million, awarded a cash bonus of $6.5 million, and granted 1.2 million stock options during fiscal 2001, the year before the manipulation was uncovered.[4]

- The CEO sold back 2.5 million shares to the company—94 percent of his total holdings—just weeks before the firm revealed that regulatory changes would significantly hurt earnings, causing the company's share price to plummet.[5]
- Former Chief Financial Officer (CFO) Weston L. Smith and other senior executives pleaded guilty to a scheme to artificially inflate financial results.[6]
- The CEO was found guilty of civil charges brought by shareholders in a derivative lawsuit and ordered to pay the company $2.88 billion in restitution.[7]

What was the board of directors doing during this period?

- The compensation committee met only *once* during 2001.[8]
- *Forbes* wrote that the CEO has "provided subpar returns to shareholders while earning huge sums for [himself]. Still, the board doesn't toss [him] out."[9]

What was the external auditor (Ernst & Young) doing?

- The audit committee met only *once* during 2001.[10]
- The president and CFO both previously were employed as auditors for Ernst & Young.
- The company paid Ernst & Young $2.5 million in consulting and other fees while also paying $1.2 million for auditing services.[11]

What were the analysts doing?

- A UBS analyst had a "strong buy" recommendation on HealthSouth.
- UBS earned $7 million in investment banking fees for services provided to the company.[12]

Perhaps not surprisingly, the CEO also received backdated stock options during his tenure—stock options whose grant dates were retroactively changed to coincide with low points in the company's stock price (see Figure 1).

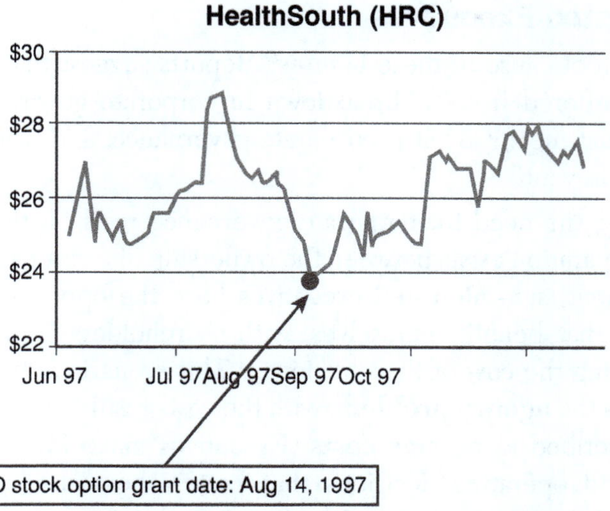

Source: Chart prepared by David F. Larcker and Brian Tayan (2010).

Figure 1 HealthSouth: CEO stock option grant date.

Interestingly, Scrushy was not convicted of accounting manipulations in a criminal trial brought by the U.S. Justice Department. However, he was ordered to pay $2.9 billion in a civil suit and, separately, was sentenced to seven years in prison for bribing a former Alabama governor.

As the case of HealthSouth illustrates, the system of checks and balances meant to prevent abuse by senior executives does not always function properly. Unfortunately, governance failures are not isolated instances. In recent years, several corporations have collapsed in prominent fashion, including American International Group, Adelphia, Bear Stearns, Enron, Global Crossing, Lehman Brothers, Tyco, and WorldCom. This list does not even include the dozens of lesser-known companies that did not make the front page of the *Wall Street Journal* or *Financial Times,* but whose owners also suffered. Furthermore, this problem is not limited to U.S. corporations. Major international companies such as Ahold, Parmalat, Royal Dutch/Shell, Satyam, and Siemens were all plagued by scandal that involved a breakdown of management oversight. Foreign companies listed on U.S. exchanges are as likely to restate their financial results as domestic companies, indicating that governance is a global issue.

Self-Interested Executives

What is the root cause of these failures? Reports suggest that these companies suffered from a "breakdown in corporate governance." What does that mean? What is corporate governance, and what is it expected to prevent?

In theory, the need for corporate governance rests on the idea that when separation exists between the ownership of a company and its management, self-interested executives have the opportunity to take actions that benefit themselves, with shareholders and stakeholders bearing the cost of these actions.[13] This scenario is typically referred to as the **agency problem**, with the costs resulting from this problem described as **agency costs**. Executives make investment, financing, and operating decisions that better themselves at the expense of other parties related to the firm.[14] To lessen agency costs, some type of control or monitoring system is put in place in the organization. That system of checks and balances is called **corporate governance**.

Behavioral psychology and other social sciences have provided evidence that individuals are self-interested. In *The Economic Approach to Human Behavior*, Gary Becker (1976) applies a theory of "rational self-interest" to economics to explain human tendencies, including one to commit crime or fraud.[15] He demonstrates that, in a wide variety of settings, individuals can take actions to benefit themselves without detection and, therefore, avoid the cost of punishment. Control mechanisms are put in place in society to deter such behavior by increasing the probability of detection and shifting the risk–reward balance so that the expected payoff from crime is decreased.

Before we rely on this theory too heavily, it is important to highlight that individuals are not always uniformly and completely self-interested. Many people exhibit self-restraint on moral grounds that have little to do with economic rewards. Not all employees who are unobserved in front of an open cash box will steal from it, and not all executives knowingly make decisions that better themselves at the expense of shareholders. This is known as **moral salience**, the knowledge that certain actions are inherently wrong even if they are undetected and left unpunished. Individuals exhibit varying degrees of moral salience, depending on their personality, religious convictions, and personal and financial circumstances. Moral salience also depends on the company involved, the country of business, and the cultural norms.[16]

The need for a governance control mechanism to discourage costly, self-interested behavior therefore depends on the size of the potential agency costs, the ability of the control mechanism to mitigate agency costs, and the cost of implementing the control mechanism (see the following sidebar).

Evidence of Self-Interested Behavior

How prevalent are agency problems? Are they outlier events or an epidemic affecting the broad population? How severe are agency costs? Are they chronic and frictional or terminal and catastrophic?

To gain some insight into these questions, it is useful to consider the frequency of negative corporate events that, in whole or in part, are correlated with agency problems. However, before looking at the statistics, we also need to highlight that not all bad outcomes are caused by self-seeking behavior. A bad outcome might well occur even though the managerial decision was appropriate (that is, other management might have made the same decision when provided with the same information). With that important caveat, consider the following descriptive statistics:

- **Bankruptcy**—Between 2000 and 2005, 1,009 publicly traded companies filed for Chapter 11 bankruptcy protection in the United States.[17] Of these, approximately 10 percent were subject to a Securities and Exchange Commission (SEC) enforcement action for violating SEC or federal rules, implying that some form of fraud played a part in the bankruptcy.[18] Bankruptcies linked to fraud are a severe case of agency problems, usually resulting in a complete loss of capital for shareholders and a significant loss for creditors.
- **Financial restatement**—Between 2004 and 2008, approximately 8 percent of publicly traded companies in the United States had to restate their financial results.[19] Although some financial restatements result from honest procedural errors in

applying accounting standards, financial restatements also can occur when senior management manipulates reported earnings for personal gain. According to Glass Lewis, the average market-adjusted two-day return for companies announcing a restatement was approximately –0.5 percent. In the case of "severe restatements" (classified as those affecting revenue recognition, core earnings, or involving fraud), share losses were –1.5 percent to –2.0 percent. Losses persist well beyond the announcement period, suggesting a material long-term impairment of shareholder value (see Figure 2).

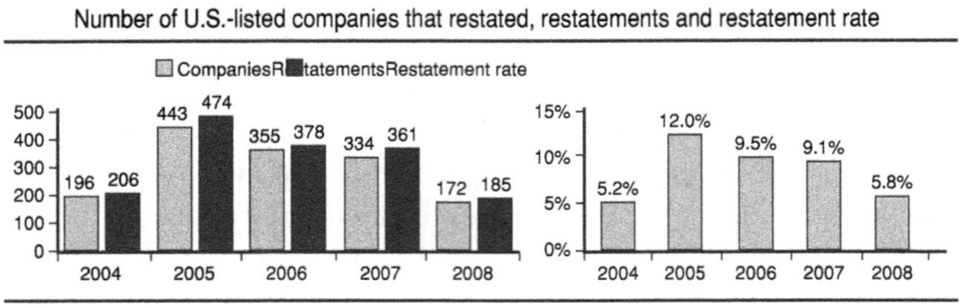

Source: Mark Grothe and Poonam Goyal (2009).

Figure 2 Restatements in the United States

- **Class action lawsuits**—Between 1996 and 2008, almost 200 class-action lawsuits were filed annually against corporate officers and directors for securities fraud. No doubt, some of this litigation was frivolous. However, market capitalization losses for defendant firms totaled approximately $130 billion each year (measured as the change in market capitalization during the class period). Although this is a somewhat crude approximation, this averages $677 million per company (see Figure 3).

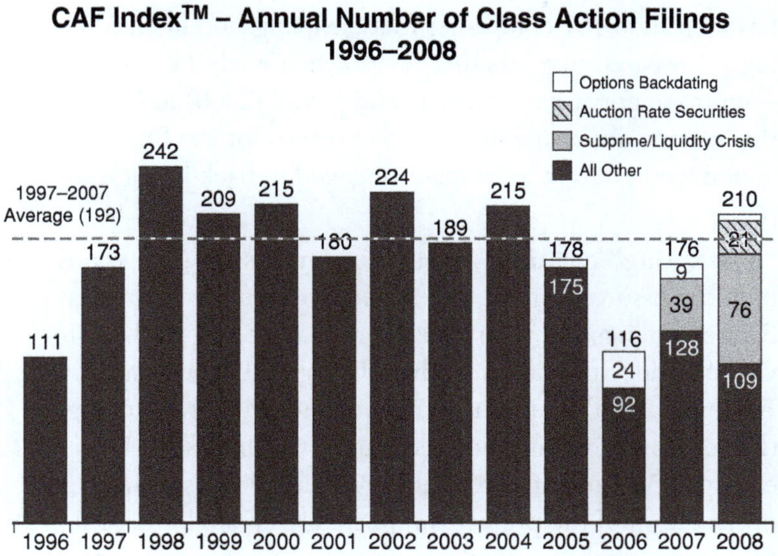

Source: *Securities Class Action Filings 2008: A Year in Review,* Cornerstone Research.

Figure 3 Annual number of class action filings (1996–2008)

- **Foreign Corrupt Practices Act violations**—The Foreign Corrupt Practices Act (FCPA) of 1977 makes it illegal for a company to offer payments to foreign officials for the purpose of obtaining or retaining business, to fail to keep accurate records of transactions, or to fail to maintain effective controls to detect potential violations of the FCPA. Between 2004 and 2008, the SEC and the U.S. Department of Justice filed approximately 20 enforcement actions per year against U.S. listed corporations for alleged FCPA violations. Notably, this figure has trended upward. Violations are settled through a disgorgement of profits and other penalties. In 2008, the SEC enforced more than $380 million in disgorgements, a record amount.[20]
- **Stock option backdating**—Backdated stock options are those whose grant dates have been retroactively changed to coincide with a relative low in the company's share price. This practice reduces the strike price of the option and increases the potential payoff to its recipient. The *Wall Street Journal*

has identified 167 companies that have engaged in backdating.[21] Research suggests that the practice might have been even more pervasive.[22] Bernile and Jarrell (2009) found that the average abnormal stock market return for the first announcement that a company engaged in backdating is –7 percent.[23]

- **"Massaging" earnings**—Senior executives are under considerable pressure from the investment community to forecast future earnings and then to deliver on those targets. In a survey of senior financial executives, Graham, Harvey, and Rajgopal (2006) found that a majority are willing to massage the company's earnings to meet quarterly forecasts.[24] For example, 55 percent state that they would delay starting a new project, even if the project is expected to create long-term value. Separately, respondents were given a scenario in which initiating a new project would cause earnings per share in the current quarter to come in \$0.10 lower. The respondents reported an 80 percent probability that they would accept the project if doing so enabled them to still meet their earnings target, but only a 60 percent probability if the project caused them to miss their earnings target.

These statistics suggest that agency problems caused by self-interested executives are likely to be quite prevalent, and the cost of managerial self-interest can be substantial.

Defining Corporate Governance

We define **corporate governance** as the collection of control mechanisms that an organization adopts to prevent or dissuade potentially self-interested managers from engaging in activities detrimental to the welfare of shareholders and stakeholders. At a minimum, the monitoring system consists of a board of directors to oversee management and an external auditor to express an opinion on the reliability of financial statements. In most cases, however, governance systems are influenced by a much broader group of constituents, including owners of the firm, creditors, labor unions, customers, suppliers, investment analysts, the media, and regulators (see Figure 4).

Introduction to Corporate Governance

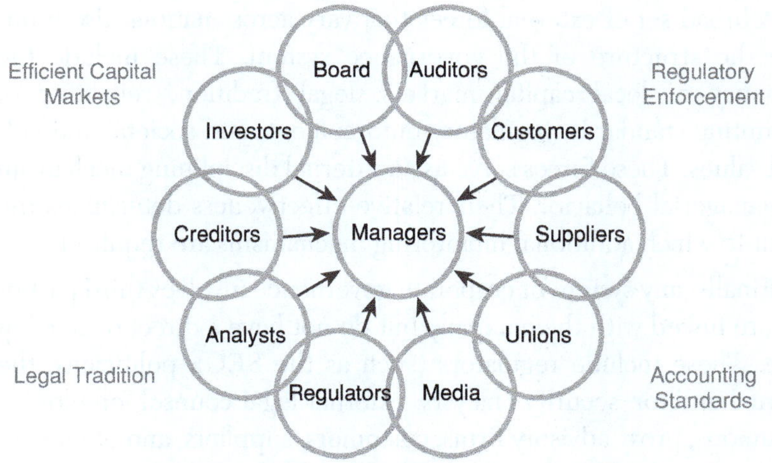

Source: Chart prepared by David F. Larcker and Brian Tayan (2011).

Figure 4 Selected determinants and participants in corporate governance systems.

For a governance system to be economically efficient, it should decrease agency costs more than the costs of implementation. However, because implementation costs are greater than zero, even the best corporate governance system will not make the cost of the agency problem disappear completely.

The structure of the governance system also depends on the fundamental orientation of the firm and the role that the firm plays in society. From a **shareholder perspective** (the viewpoint that the primary obligation of the organization is to maximize shareholder value), effective corporate governance should increase the value of equity holders by better aligning incentives between management and shareholders. From a **stakeholder perspective** (the viewpoint that the organization has a societal obligation beyond increasing shareholder value), effective governance should support policies that produce stable and safe employment, provide an acceptable standard of living to workers, mitigate risk for debt holders, and improve the community and environment.[25] Obviously, the governance system that maximizes shareholder value might not be the same as the one that maximizes stakeholder value.

A broad set of external forces that vary across nations also influence the structure of the governance system. These include the efficiency of local capital markets, legal tradition, reliability of accounting standards, regulatory enforcement, and societal and cultural values. These forces serve as an external disciplining mechanism on managerial behavior. Their relative effectiveness determines the extent to which additional monitoring mechanisms are required.

Finally, any system of corporate governance involves third parties that are linked with the company but do not have a direct ownership stake. These include regulators (such as the SEC), politicians, the external auditor, security analysts, external legal counsel, employees and unions, proxy advisory firms, customers, suppliers, and other similar participants. Third parties might be subject to their own agency issues that compromise their ability to work solely in the interest of the company. For example, the external auditor is employed by an accounting firm that seeks to improve its own financial condition; when the accounting firm also provides non-audit services, the auditor *might* be confronted with conflicting objectives. Likewise, security analysts are employed by investment firms that serve both institutional and retail clients; when the analyst covers a company that is also a client of the investment firm, the analyst might face added pressure by his firm to publish positive comments about the company that are misleading to shareholders. These types of conflicts can contribute to a breakdown in oversight of management activity.

Corporate Governance Standards

There are no universally agreed-upon standards that determine good governance. Still, this has not stopped blue-ribbon panels from recommending uniform standards to market participants. For example, in December 1992, the Cadbury Committee—commissioned by the British government "to help raise the standards of corporate governance and the level of confidence in financial reporting and auditing"—issued a *Code of Best Practices* that, in many ways, provided a benchmark set of recommendations on governance.[26] Key recommendations included separating the chairman and chief executive officer titles, appointing independent directors, reducing conflicts of interest at the board level because of business or other relationships, convening an independent audit committee, and reviewing the effectiveness of the company's internal controls. These standards set the basis for listing requirements on the London Stock Exchange and were largely adopted by the New York Stock Exchange (NYSE). However, compliance with these standards has not always translated into effective governance. For example, Enron was compliant with NYSE requirements, including requirements to have a majority of independent directors and fully independent audit and compensation committees, yet it still failed along many legal and ethical dimensions.

Over time, a series of formal regulations and informal guidelines has been proposed to address perceived shortcomings in governance systems as they are exposed. One of the most important pieces of formal legislation relating to governance is the Sarbanes–Oxley Act of 2002 (SOX). Primarily a reaction to the failures of Enron and others, SOX mandated a series of requirements to improve corporate controls and reduce conflicts of interest. Importantly, CEOs and CFOs found to have made material misrepresentations in the financial statements are now subject to criminal penalties. Despite these efforts, corporate failures stemming from deficient governance systems continue. In 2005, Refco, a large U.S.-based foreign exchange and commodity broker, filed for bankruptcy after revealing that it had hidden $430 million in loans made to its CEO.[27] The disclosure came just two months after the firm raised $583 million in an initial public offering. That same year, mortgage guarantor Fannie Mae announced that it had overstated earnings by $6.3 billion because it had misapplied more than 20 accounting standards relating to loans, investment securities, and derivatives. Insufficient capital levels eventually led the company to seek conservatorship by the U.S. government.[28]

In 2009, Sen. Charles Schumer of New York proposed new legislation to stem the tide of governance collapses. Known as the Shareholder's Bill of Rights, the legislation stipulated that companies adopt procedural changes designed to give shareholders greater influence over director elections and compensation. Requirements included a shift toward annual elections for all directors (thereby disallowing staggered or classified boards), a standard of majority voting for director elections (instead of plurality voting) in which directors in uncontested elections must resign if they do not receive a majority vote, the right for certain institutional shareholders to directly nominate board candidates on the company proxy (proxy access), the separation of the chairman and CEO roles, and the right for shareholders to have an advisory vote on executive compensation (say-on-pay). The 2010 Dodd–Frank Wall Street Reform and Consumer Protection Act subsequently adopted several of these recommendations, including proxy access and say-on-pay. The interesting question is whether this legislation is a product of political expediency or actually is based on rigorous theory and empirical research.[29]

Several third-party organizations, such as The Corporate Library and Risk Metrics Group/Institutional Shareholder Services (ISS), attempt to protect investors from inadequate corporate governance by publishing governance ratings on individual companies. These rating agencies use alphanumeric or numeric systems that rank companies according to a set of criteria that they believe measure governance effectiveness. Companies with high ratings are considered less risky and most likely to grow shareholder value. Companies with low ratings are considered more risky and have the highest potential for failure or fraud. However, the accuracy and predictive power of these ratings has not been clearly demonstrated. Critics allege that ratings encourage a "check-the-box" approach to governance that overlooks important context. The potential shortcomings of these ratings were spotlighted in the case of HealthSouth. Before evidence of earnings manipulation was brought to light, the company had a RiskMetrics/ISS rating that placed it in the top 35 percent of Standard & Poor's 500 companies and the top 8 percent of its industry peers.[30]

Changes in the business environment further complicate attempts to identify uniform standards of governance. Some recent trends include the increased prominence of private equity, activist investors, and proxy advisory firms in the governance space.

- **Private equity**—Private equity firms implement governance systems that are considerably different from those at most public companies. Publicly owned companies must demonstrate independence at the board level, but private equity–owned companies operate with very low levels of independence (almost everyone on the board has a relationship to the company and has a vested interest in its operations). Private equity companies also offer extremely high compensation to senior executives, a practice that is criticized among public companies but one that is strictly tied to the creation of economic value. Should public companies adopt certain aspects from the private equity model of governance? Would this produce more or less shareholder value?

- **Activist investors**—Institutional investors, hedge funds, and pension funds have become considerably more active in attempting to influence management and the board through the annual proxy voting process. Are the interests of these parties consistent with those of individual shareholders? Does public debate between these parties reflect a movement toward improved dialogue about corporate objectives and strategy? Or does it constitute an unnecessary intrusion by activists who have their own self-interested agendas?
- **Proxy advisory firms**—Recent SEC rules require that mutual funds disclose how they vote their annual proxies.[31] These rules have coincided with increased media attention on the voting process, which was previously considered a formality of little interest. Has the disclosure of voting improved corporate governance? At the same time, these rules have stimulated demand for commercial firms—such as RiskMetrics/ISS and Glass Lewis—to provide recommendations on how to vote on proxy proposals. What is the impact of shareholders relying on third parties to inform their voting decisions? Are the recommendations of these firms consistent with good governance?

Best Practice or Best Practices? Does "One Size Fit All?"

It is highly unlikely that a single set of best practices exists for all firms, despite the attempts of some to impose uniform standards. Governance is a complex and dynamic system that involves the interaction of a diverse set of constituents, all of whom play a role in monitoring executive behavior. Because of this complexity, it is difficult to assess the impact of a single component. Focusing an analysis on one or two mechanisms without considering the broader context can be a prescription for failure. For example, is it sufficient to insist that a company separate the chairman and CEO positions without considering who the CEO is and other structural, cultural, and governance features of the company?

Applying a "one-size-fits-all" approach to governance can lead to incorrect conclusions and is unlikely to substantially improve corporate performance. The standards most often associated with good governance might appear to be good ideas, but when applied universally, they can result in failure as often as success. For example, consider the idea of board independence. Is a board consisting primarily of independent directors superior to a board comprised entirely of internal directors? How should individual attributes such as their business acumen, professional background, ethical standards of responsibility, level of engagement, relationship with the CEO, and reliance on director fees to maintain their standard of living factor into our analysis?[32] Personal attributes might influence independence of perspective more than predetermined standards.[33] However, these elements are rarely captured in regulatory requirements.[34]

In governance, context matters. A set of governance mechanisms that works well in one setting might prove disastrous in another. This situation becomes apparent when considering international governance systems. For example, Germany requires labor union representation on many corporate boards. How effective would such a system be in the United States? Japanese boards have few outside directors, and many of those who are outside directors come from banks that provide capital to the firm or key customers and suppliers. What would be the impact on Japanese companies if they were required to adopt the independence standards of the United States? These are difficult questions, but ones that investors must consider when deciding where to allocate their investment dollars.

Relationship between Corporate Governance and Firm Performance

According to a 2002 survey by McKinsey & Company, nearly 80 percent of institutional investors responded that they would pay a premium for a well-governed company. The size of the premium varied by market, ranging from 11 percent for a company in Canada to around 40 percent for a company in Morocco, Egypt, or Russia (see Figure 5).[35] These results imply that investors perceive well-governed companies to be better investments than poorly governed companies.[36] They are also consistent with the idea that governance systems are more important in certain countries than in others.

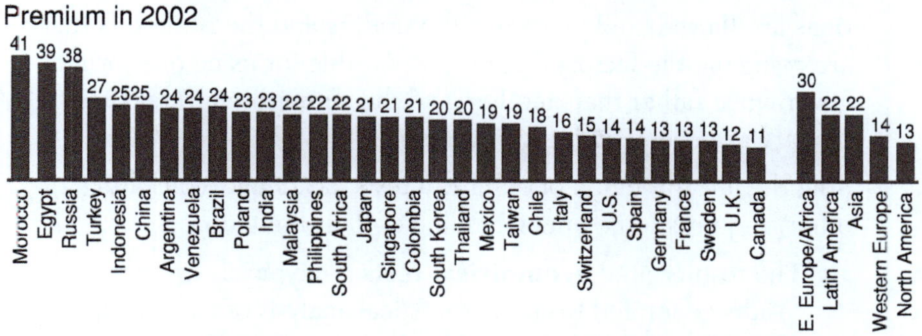

Source: Paul Coombes and Mark Watson (2002). "Global Investor Opinion Survey 2002: Key Findings." McKinsey & Company.

Figure 5 Indicated premiums for good corporate governance, by country.

Many studies link measures of corporate governance with firm operating and stock price performance. Perhaps the most widely cited study was done by Gompers, Ishii, and Metrick (2003).[37] They found that companies that employ "shareholder-friendly" governance features significantly outperform companies that employ "shareholder unfriendly" governance features. This is an important research study but these results are not completely definitive. Currently, researchers have not produced a reliable litmus test that measures overall governance quality.

Interpreting Empirical Research

Oliver Williamson, winner of the 2009 Nobel Prize in Economics, observed the following:

"I have no doubt that the economics of governance is influential in significant measure because it does speak to real-world phenomena and invites *empirical testing* .... All feasible forms of organizations are flawed, and ... we need to understand the trade-offs that are going on, the factors that are responsible for using one form of governance rather than another, and the strengths and weaknesses that are associated with each of them."[39]

Still, the interpretation of empirical tests (academic, consulting, or other) requires some understanding of their limitations:

1. The results cited in **empirical tests** are typically average results generated from the statistical analysis of large samples of firms. Large samples enable a researcher to identify trends that are generally prevalent across companies. However, they do not tell us what we can expect to find at a specific company. Case or field studies can help answer firm-specific questions, but their results are difficult to generalize because they are based on only a handful of firms that may not be typical of the general population of firms.

2. Empirical tests can identify associations between variables, but they do not demonstrate causality. This is a recurring problem in nonexperimental social science. If we observe a negative stock price return when a company adopts a governance change, it does not tell us that the change caused the stock price decline. It is possible that another (exogenous) factor might have been the cause. Ideally, we would control for this by observing what would have happened had another action been taken (the counterfactual outcome); however, this is impossible to observe. In corporate governance, we do not have the luxury of controlled samples. Still, empirical results are superior to guesswork or intuition.
3. The performance metrics that governance researchers typically use fall into two broad categories: operating metrics and stock price metrics. Operating metrics (such as return on assets and operating cash flow) are somewhat backward looking but are generally considered to provide insight into value changes within the firm. Stock price metrics are typically based on **abnormal** or **excess** returns (the so-called **alpha**, calculated as observed returns minus the expected returns, given the risk of the stock). Assuming reasonably efficient markets, excess returns provide a measure of change in economic value for shareholders. The researcher must determine which metric is better for evaluating the question at hand. The choice will depend on whether the market should be able to anticipate the impact of interest.
4. Another metric that is commonly used in governance research is the ratio of market-to-book value (sometimes referred to as **Tobin's Q** or simply **Q**). Q is based on the theory that a firm with superior performance will trade in the market at a valuation that is higher than the accounting value of its net assets. While this may be true, we view Q to be an ambiguous measure of firm performance and inferior to traditional operating metrics and excess stock price returns.

5. We sometimes refer to **event studies**. Event studies measure the stock market's reaction to news or events. These studies have validity only to the extent that the reader believes that markets are at least partly efficient. Even if so, event studies cannot easily control for confounding events (such as other news released by the company during the measurement period). Moreover, event studies require the researcher to make important risk adjustments when computing excess stock returns. Although several risk adjustments have become "accepted," their computation is complex, and it is difficult to know whether the researcher made them properly.

Endnotes

1. Some material in this chapter is adapted from David F. Larcker and Brian Tayan, "Models of Corporate Governance: Who's the Fairest of Them All?" Stanford GSB Case No. CG 11, January 15, 2008. See https://gsbapps.stanford.edu/cases/detail1.asp?Document_ID=3054. Copyright 2008 by the Board of Trustees of the Leland Stanford Junior University. All rights reserved. Used with permission from the Stanford University Graduate School of Business.

2. See Aaron Beam and Chris Warner, *HealthSouth: The Wagon to Disaster* (Fairhope, AL: Wagon Publishing, 2009).

3. Lisa Fingeret Roth, "HealthSouth CFO Admits Fraud Charges," FT.com (March 26, 2003). See http://proquest.umi.com/pqdweb?did=318664941&sid=1&Fmt=3&clientId=12498&RQT=309&VName=PQD.

4. HealthSouth Corporation, Form DEF14-A, filed with the Securities and Exchange Commission, May 16, 2002.

5. In re: HealthSouth Corporation Bondholder Litigation. United States District Court Northern District of Alabama Southern Division. Master File No. CV-03-BE-1500-S.

6. Chad Terhune and Carrick Mollenkamp, "HealthSouth Officials May Sign Plea Agreements—Moves by Finance Executives Would Likely Help Build Criminal Case Against CEO," *Wall Street Journal* (March 26, 2003, Eastern edition): A.14.

7. Carrick Mollenkamp, "Some of Scrushy's Lawyers Ask Others on Team for Money Back," *Wall Street Journal* (December 17, 2003, Eastern edition): A.16.

8. HealthSouth Corporation, Form DEF14-A.

9. Dan Ackman, "CEO Compensation for Life?" Forbes.com (April 25, 2002). Accessed November 16, 2010. www.forbes.com/2002/04/25/0425ceotenure.html.

10. HealthSouth Corporation, Form DEF14-A. See also Jonathan Weil and Cassell Bryan-Low, "Questioning the Books: Audit Committee Met Only Once During 2001," *Wall Street Journal* (March 21, 2003, Eastern edition): A.2.

11. HealthSouth Corporation, Form DEF14-A.

12. Ken Brown and Robert Frank, "Analyst's Bullishness on HealthSouth's Stock Didn't Waver," *Wall Street Journal* (April 4, 2003, Eastern edition): C.1.

13. This issue was the basis of the classic discussion in Adolph Berle and Gardiner Means, *The Modern Corporation and Private Property* (New York: Harcourt, Brace, and World, 1932).

14. The phrase *rent extraction* is another commonly used term for agency costs and refers to economic costs taken out of the system without any corresponding contribution in productivity.

15. Gary Becker, *The Economic Approach to Human Behavior* (Chicago: University of Chicago Press, 1976).

16. For example, a study by Boivie, Lange, McDonald, and Westphal found that CEOs who strongly identify with their company are less likely to accept expensive perquisites or make other decisions that are at odds with shareholder interests. Source: Steven Boivie, Donald Lange, Michael L. McDonald, and James D. Westphal, "Me or We: The Effects of CEO Organizational Identification of Agency Costs," *Academy of Management Proceedings* (2009): 1-6.

17. Deloitte, "Ten Things about Bankruptcy and Fraud: A Review of Bankruptcy Filings," Deloitte Forensic Center (2008). See www.deloitte.com/view/en_US/us/Services/Financial-Advisory-Services/Forensic-Center/1d42a68c4d101210VgnVCM100000ba42f00aRCRD.htm.

18. Enforcement actions are measured as the number of Accounting and Auditing Enforcement Releases (AAER) by the SEC. The SEC issues an AAER for alleged violations of SEC and federal rules. Academic researchers have used AAER as a proxy for severe fraud because most companies that commit financial statement fraud receive SEC enforcement actions.

19. Mark Grothe, "The Errors of Their Ways," Yellow Card Trend Report, Glass Lewis & Co. (February 27, 2007).

20. David C. Weiss, "The Foreign Corrupt Practices Act, SEC Disgorgement of Profits, and the Evolving International Bribery Regime: Weighing Proportionality, Retribution, and Deterrence," *Michigan Journal of International Law* 30 (2009): 147. See www.heinonline.org/HOL/Page?handle=hein.journals/mjil30&id=1&size=2&collection=journals&index=journals/mjil.

21. Anonymous, "Perfect Payday: Options Scorecard," Wall Street Journal Online (2007). See http://online.wsj.com/public/resources/documents/info-optionsscore06-full.html.

22. Erik Lie, "On the Timing of CEO Stock Option Awards," *Management Science* 51 (2005): 802–812. Lucian A. Bebchuk, Yaniv Grinstein, and Urs C. Peyer. "Lucky CEOs and Lucky Directors," *Journal of Finance* 65 (2010): 2,363–2,401.

23. Gennaro Bernile and Gregg A. Jarrell, "The Impact of the Options Backdating Scandal on Shareholders," *Journal of Accounting and Economics* 47 (2009): 1–2. Also Accounting Research on Issues of Contemporary Interest (March 2009): 2-26.

24. John Graham, Campbell Harvey, and Shiva Rajgopal, "Value Destruction and Financial Reporting Decisions," *Financial Analysts Journal* 62 (2006): 27–39.

25. The cost–benefit assessment of a governance system also depends on whether the company operates under a shareholder-centric or stakeholder-centric model. The fundamentally different orientation of these models makes it difficult for an outside observer to compare their effectiveness. For example, a decision to maximize shareholder value might come at the cost of the employee and environmental objectives of stakeholders, but comparing these costs is not easy.

26. Cadbury Committee, *Report of the Committee on the Financial Aspects of Corporate Governance* (London: Gee, 1992).

27. Deborah Solomon, Carrick Mollenkamp, Peter A. McKay, and Jonathan Weil, "Refco's Debts Started with Several Clients; Bennett Secretly Intervened to Assume Some Obligations; Return of Victor Niederhoffer," *Wall Street Journal* (October 21, 2005, Eastern edition): C1.

28. James R. Hagerty, "Politics & Economics: Fannie Mae Moves Toward Resolution with Restatement," *Wall Street Journal* (December 7, 2006, Eastern edition) A.4. Damian Paletta, "Fannie Sues KPMG for $2 Billion Over Costs of Accounting Issues," *Wall Street Journal* (December 13, 2006, Eastern edition): A.16.

29. A forthcoming study by Larcker, Ormazabal, and Taylor found that the legislative provisions in Schumer and Dodd–Frank are associated with negative stock price returns for affected companies. These results seemed to have little impact on the congressional debate. Similarly, the legislators who drafted the Sarbanes–Oxley Act of 2002 did not take into account research literature. See David F. Larcker, Gaizka Ormazabal, and Daniel J. Taylor, "The Market Reaction to Corporate Governance Regulation," *Journal of Financial Economics* (forthcoming); and Roberta Romano, "The Sarbanes–Oxley Act and the Making of Quack Corporate Governance," *Yale Law Review* 114 (2005): 1,521–1,612.

30. Cited in Jeffrey Sonnenfeld, "Good Governance and the Misleading Myths of Bad Metrics," *Academy of Management Executive* 18 (2001): 108–113.

31. Securities Lawyer's Deskbook. "Investment Company Act of 1940. Rule 30b1-4," *The University of Cincinnati College of Law*. See www.law.uc.edu/CCL/InvCoRls/rule30b1-4.html. See also "Report of Proxy Voting, Record Disclosure of Proxy Voting Policies, and Proxy Voting Records by Registered Management Investment Companies," Securities and Exchange Commission: 17 CFR Parts 239, 249, 270, and 274 Release Nos. 33-8188, 34-47304, IC-25922; File No. S7-36-02. www.sec.gov/rules/final/33-8188.htm.

32. The NYSE acknowledges this risk.

33. Sonnenfeld has written, "At least as important are the human dynamics of boards as social systems where leadership character, individual values, decision-making processes, conflict management, and strategic thinking will truly differentiate a firm's governance." Jeffrey Sonnenfeld, "Good Governance and the Misleading Myths of Bad Metrics," *Academy of Management Executive* 18 (2004): 108–113.

34. Milton Harris and Artur Ravi, "A Theory of Board Control and Size," *Review of Financial Studies* 21 (2008): 1,797–1,831.

35. Paul Coombes and Mark Watson, "Global Investor Opinion Survey 2002: Key Findings," McKinsey & Co. (2002). Accessed November 1, 2010. See www.mckinsey.com/clientservice/organizationleadership/service/corpgovernance/pdf/globalinvestoropinionsurvey2002.pdf.

36. This is what investors say they would do when asked in a formal survey. However, this study does not provide evidence that investors actually take governance into account when making investment decisions.

37. Paul Gompers, Joy Ishii, and Andrew Metrick, "Corporate Governance and Equity Prices," *Quarterly Journal of Economics* 118 (2003): 107–155.

38. We are not attempting to provide a complete and comprehensive review of the research literature. Our goal is to select specific papers that provide a fair reflection of general research results.

39. Emphasis added. Nobel Prize Organization, "Oliver E. Williamson—Interview" (2009). See http://nobelprize.org/nobel_prizes/economics/laureates/2009/williamson-telephone.html.

Board of Directors: Duties and Liability

In this chapter, we examine the duties and liabilities that come with directorship. We start with an overview of the role of the board and the requirement for independence. We then review the basic operations of the board. This includes evaluating the process by which topics are selected, deliberated, and decided. Next, we review the process by which directors are elected and removed. Finally, we examine the legal responsibilities that come with directorship and consider the potential liability directors face when they fail to uphold their duties. While we focus on boards of U.S. corporations, the broad principles apply to boards in all countries.

Board Responsibilities

In a document called Principles of Corporate Governance, the Organization for Economic Cooperation and Development (OECD) lays out a vision of the responsibilities of the board:

> The corporate governance framework should ensure the strategic guidance of the company, the effective monitoring of management by the board, and the board's accountability to the company and the shareholders.[1]

That is, the board is expected to provide both advisory and oversight functions. Although these responsibilities are linked in many ways, they have fundamentally different focuses. In an **advisory** capacity, the board consults with management regarding the strategic and operational direction of the company. Attention is paid to decisions that balance risk and reward. Board members are selected based on the skill and expertise they offer for this purpose, including previous experience in a relevant industry or function.

In its **oversight** capacity, the board is expected to monitor management and ensure that it is acting diligently in the interests of shareholders. The board hires and fires the chief executive officer, measures corporate performance, evaluates management contribution to performance, and awards compensation. It also oversees legal and regulatory compliance, including the audit process, reporting requirements for publicly traded companies, and industry-specific regulations. In fulfilling these responsibilities, the board often relies on the advice of legal counsel and other paid professionals, such as external auditors, executive recruiters, compensation consultants, investment bankers, and tax advisors. Effective board members are individuals that can capably complete both advisory and oversight responsibilities.

The responsibilities of directors are separate and distinct from those of management. Directors are expected to advise on corporate strategy but do not develop the strategy. They are expected to ensure the integrity of the financial statements but do not prepare the statements themselves. The board is not an extension of management. The board is a governing body elected to represent the interests of shareholders.

Survey data suggests that board members understand the role they are expected to serve. When asked to describe what areas directors should pay most attention to, other than profitability and shareholder value, directors list future growth, risk management, and development of human capital as their top three priorities. Other areas of focus include cultural development, executive compensation, and regulatory compliance.[2] Still, some evidence indicates that directors prefer the advisory function to the monitoring function. When asked what issues they would like to spend more time discussing, directors list strategic planning, competition, and succession planning among their top responses. By contrast, most want to spend the same or less time on executive compensation, monitoring performance, and compliance and regulatory issues.[3]

Board Independence

To be effective in an advisory and oversight capacity, board members are expected to exhibit independence. From a regulatory standpoint, independence is evaluated by the degree to which a director is free from conflicts of interest that might compromise his or her ability to act solely in the interest of the firm. Independence is critical in that it ensures that directors are able to take positions in opposition to those of management when necessary. In the United States, the New York Stock Exchange (NYSE) requires that listed companies have a majority of independent directors. It also requires solely independent audit, compensation, and nominating and governance committees.

However, regulatory standards are not necessarily the same as true independence. Board members who have worked with management over a long period of time may well form ties that will challenge a truly independent perspective. Independence may also be compromised by individual factors, such as the board member's background, education, experience, values, and personal relation to management. There are many examples of boards comprised of highly capable directors who went along with management decisions that later proved disastrous. For example, the board of Enron failed to rein in management actions that were later held to be criminal. Similarly, the board of Disney acquiesced to management in the hiring and firing of Michael Ovitz, which later drew harsh criticism from shareholders.

Anecdotal evidence suggests that board members do not necessarily believe that formal independence standards are correlated with true independence. An informal study conducted by professors at Harvard Business School found that relevant experience is a more important indicator of director quality than regulatory requirements. According to one respondent, "I don't think independence is anywhere near as important as people thought it was. ... It was a red herring."[4] Nevertheless, most directors believe that they are capable of maintaining independence. In a survey by *Corporate Board Member* magazine, 85 percent of directors responded that they and their fellow board members effectively challenged management when necessary.[5]

The Operations of the Board

A chairman presides over meetings of the board of directors. The chairman is responsible for setting the agenda, scheduling meetings, and coordinating actions of board committees. As such, the chairman holds considerable sway over the governance process by determining the content and timing of matters brought before the board.

Traditionally, the CEO has served as the chairman of the board in most U.S. corporations. In recent years, however, it has become more common for a nonexecutive director to serve as chair. Given the advising and oversight responsibilities of the board, several obvious conflicts could arise from a dual chairman/CEO. Chief among them are the commingling of responsibilities that are afforded separately to management and the board, and the potential for weakened oversight in the areas of performance evaluation, compensation, succession planning, and recruitment of independent directors. At the same time, a dual chairman/CEO offers potential benefits regarding singular leadership within the organization and clear, efficient decision making.

In the debate over the Sarbanes-Oxley Act of 2002 (SOX), Congress considered but ultimately rejected calls to require an independent director to serve as chairman. Instead, SOX required that companies designate an independent director as "lead director" for each board meeting. The lead director may be named to serve on a meeting-by-meeting basis or may be appointed to serve continuously until replaced. The role of the lead director is to represent the independent directors in conversations with the CEO. This structure is intended to fortify an independent review of management among companies with a dual chairman/CEO.

Board actions take place either at board meetings or by written consent. At a board meeting, resolutions are presented to the board and voted upon. An action is complete when it receives a majority of votes in support. When the board acts by **written consent**, a written resolution is circulated among board members for their signatures. The action is complete when a majority of the directors have signed the document. Because board actions by written consent do not require advance notice, they can occur more quickly than actions taken at board meetings.

In addition to attending meetings of the full board, independent directors meet at least once a year in **executive session**, in which executive directors are not present. This practice was mandated by SOX. While no formal actions are taken at these meetings, executive sessions give outside directors an opportunity to discuss candidly the performance of management, operating results, internal controls, and succession planning. The lead independent director presides over these meetings.

Directors report spending approximately 20 hours per month on board matters. A typical meeting lasts between two and six hours, but some last as long as eight hours. Increased regulatory requirements in recent years have done much to lengthen board meetings. Still, most directors believe that the agenda is structured to make efficient use of their time and that 20 hours per month is sufficient to satisfy their duties.[6]

To inform its decisions, the board relies on materials provided by management. Survey data indicates that the quality of this information might not be adequate. For example, a study by Deloitte Consulting found that although 91 percent of directors reported receiving good or excellent information about their company's financial results, only 61 percent were satisfied with the information they received on operational performance. Additionally, fewer than half believed they were receiving excellent or good information about important areas of the business, including product quality, product innovation, relationships with business partners and suppliers, customer satisfaction, and employee commitment.[7] Nonexecutive directors can address these deficiencies by requesting that management improve reporting on nonfinancial as well as financial strategic performance measures. Directors may also benefit through more direct contact with management. According to one director, "There is no substitute for time spent meeting with management of the different divisions or sectors that are the next level down the corporate ladder, having them present directly to the board, [and] visiting operations."[8]

Board Committees

Not all corporate matters are deliberated by the full board of directors. Some are delegated to committees. These committees can be standing or *ad hoc*, depending on the nature of the topic. Directors are assigned to committees based on their qualifications. On important matters, such as the design and approval of executive compensation contracts, recommendations of the committee are brought before the full board for a vote.

Historically, the creation of committees was left largely to the discretion of the board. The only committee that the Securities and Exchange Commission (SEC) required was an audit committee, which was mandated for all publicly listed companies in 1977. In 2002, the Sarbanes-Oxley Act required additional committees, including a compensation committee, a governance committee, and a nominating committee. The act stipulated that these committees and the audit committee consist entirely of independent directors.

The **audit committee** is responsible for overseeing the company's external audit and is the primary contact between the auditor and the company. This reporting relationship is intended to prevent management manipulation of the audit. Under SOX, the audit committee must have at least three members, all of whom are financially literate; the chair also must be a financial expert. The audit committee maintains a written charter that outlines its duties to the full board, including these obligations:

1. Overseeing the financial reporting and disclosure process
2. Monitoring the choice of accounting policies and principles
3. Overseeing the hiring, performance, and independence of the external auditor
4. Overseeing regulatory compliance, ethics, and whistleblower hotlines
5. Monitoring internal control processes
6. Overseeing the performance of the internal audit function
7. Discussing risk-management policies and practices with management[9]

According to the NACD, audit committees meet an average of seven times per year for 3.2 hours.[10] Ninety-four percent of directors believe that the audit committee is effective in its oversight of the financial reporting process.[11]

The **compensation committee** is responsible for setting the compensation of the CEO and for advising the CEO on the compensation of other senior executives. Sarbanes-Oxley established no minimum committee size. The obligations of the compensation committee include the following:

1. Setting the compensation of the CEO
2. Setting and reviewing performance-related goals for the CEO
3. Determining appropriate compensation structure for the CEO, given these performance expectations
4. Monitoring CEO performance relative to targets
5. Setting or advising the CEO on other officers' compensation
6. Advising the CEO on and overseeing compensation of nonexecutive employees
7. Setting board compensation
8. Hiring consultants to assist in the compensation process, as appropriate[12]

Compensation committees meet an average of five times per year for 2.4 hours.[13] Seventy-six percent of directors believe the compensation committee can properly manage CEO compensation.[14]

The **governance committee** is responsible for evaluating the company's governance structure and processes and recommending improvements, when appropriate. The **nominating committee** is responsible for identifying, evaluating, and nominating new directors when board seats need to be filled. The nominating committee is also typically in charge of leading the CEO succession-planning process.

In most companies, the nominating and governance committees are combined into a single committee with these responsibilities:

1. Identifying qualified individuals to serve on the board
2. Selecting nominees to be put before a shareholder vote at the annual meeting
3. Hiring consultants to assist in the director recruitment process, as appropriate
4. Determining governance standards for the corporation
5. Managing the board evaluation process
6. Managing the CEO evaluation process[15]

The nominating and governance committee meets an average of four times per year for 1.9 hours.[16] Despite the independence of this committee, the CEO often has significant input into the choice of directors nominated to the board. This is true whether or not the CEO holds the dual role of chairman.

Boards are free to establish additional committees beyond those required by listing exchanges. These committees generally monitor functional areas that the board believes to hold strategic importance for the firm, thus meriting additional oversight (**specialized committees**). According to Spencer Stuart, 34 percent of companies have a committee dedicated to finance, 11 percent to corporate social responsibility, 6 percent to science and technology, 4 percent to legal, 4 percent to the environment, and 3 percent to risk.[17] These committees oversee and advise these functions; they do not directly manage them, which is the purview of management (see the following sidebar).

Specialized Board Committees

The board of Merck & Co. convenes a Research Committee to monitor its drug discovery and development process:

"The Research Committee, which is comprised of independent directors, assists the Board in its oversight of matters pertaining to the Company's strategies and operations for the research and development of pharmaceutical products and vaccines. The Research Committee identifies areas and activities that are critical to the success of the Company's drug and vaccine discovery, development, and licensing efforts, as well as evaluates the effectiveness of the Company's drug and vaccine discovery, development, and licensing strategies and operations. The Research Committee also keeps the Board apprised of this evaluation process and findings and makes appropriate recommendations to the President of Merck Research Laboratories and to the Board on modifications of strategies and operations."[18]

Fifth Third Bancorp has a Risk and Compliance Committee that monitors financial, credit, and regulatory risk:

"The Committee oversees management's compliance with all of the Company's regulatory obligations arising under applicable federal and state banking laws, rules, and regulations, including any terms and conditions required from time to time by any action, formal or informal, of any federal or state banking regulatory agency or authority and any responses of management to any inquiries from any applicable banking regulator, and oversees management's implementation and enforcement of the Company's risk management policies and procedures."[19]

The board of Cisco Systems has an Investment and Finance Committee that monitors a broad range of financial activities:

"The Investment/Finance Committee reviews and approves Cisco's global investment policy; reviews minority investments, fixed income assets, insurance risk management policies and programs, and tax programs; oversees Cisco's stock repurchase programs; and also reviews Cisco's currency, interest rate, and equity risk management policies. This committee is also authorized to approve the issuance of debt securities, certain real estate acquisitions and leases, and charitable contributions made on behalf of Cisco."[20]

General Mills has a Public Responsibility Committee that has these functions:

- Reviews public policy and social trends affecting General Mills
- Monitors corporate citizenship activities
- Evaluates policies to ensure that they meet ethical obligations to employees, consumers, and society
- Reviews policies governing political contributions and the company's record of contributions[21]

Duration of Director Terms

Traditionally, directors are elected annually to one-year terms. In some companies, directors are elected to two- or three-year terms, with a subset of directors standing for reelection each year. Companies that follow this protocol are referred to as having **staggered** (or **classified**) boards. Under a typical staggered board, directors are elected to three-year terms, with one-third of the board standing for reelection every three years. As a result, it is not possible for the board to be ousted in a single year; two election cycles are needed for a majority of the board to turn over. Staggered boards can be an effective antitakeover protection.

Largely in response to the increased incidence of hostile takeovers in the 1980s, firms began adopting staggered boards. For example, from 1994 to 1999, the percentage of firms that adopted staggered boards at the time they went public increased from 43 percent to 82 percent in the United States.[22] In recent years, however, the trend has reversed. Companies have come under fire from shareholder activists and proxy advisory firms who believe that staggered board elections insulate directors from shareholder influence.[23] Institutional investors, particularly public pension plans, often have policies of opposing staggered boards. Some public companies have responded to shareholder pressure by destaggering their boards. In

2009, about 50 percent of publicly traded companies had staggered boards, down from 63 percent in 2002.[24]

Director Elections

In most companies, the board of directors is elected by shareholders on a one-share, one-vote basis. For example, if there are nine seats on a board, a shareholder with 100 shares can cast 100 votes for each of the nine people nominated. Shareholders who do not want to vote for one or all of the nominees can withhold votes for selected individuals. Directors win an election by obtaining a **plurality** of votes, meaning that the directors who receive the most votes win, regardless of whether they receive a majority of votes. In an uncontested election, a director is elected as long as he or she receives at least one vote.

Three main alternatives to this system of voting exist: dual-class stock, majority voting, and cumulative voting. A company with **dual-class shares** has more than one class of common stock. In general, each class has equal economic interest in the company but unequal voting rights. For example, Class A shares might be afforded one vote per share, whereas Class B shares might have ten votes per share. Typically, an insider, founding family member, or other shareholder friendly to management holds the class of shares with preferential voting rights, which gives that person significant (if not outright) influence over board elections. Dual-class stock thus tends to weaken the influence of public shareholders. Approximately 9 percent of publicly traded corporations in the United States have some form of dual-class structure.[25] Google, the New York Times Co., and Hershey all have dual-class shares.

The second variation in voting procedures is **majority voting**. Majority voting differs from plurality voting in that a director is required to receive a majority of votes to be elected. This means that even in an uncontested election, a director can fail to win a board seat if over half of all outstanding votes are withheld from him or her. The specific procedures of majority voting systems vary. In some companies, candidates who receive more withhold votes than votes in favor are strictly refused a seat on the board. More commonly, the director is required to submit a letter of resignation, and the rest of the board has discretion over whether to accept it. Other companies require resignation, but only after a replacement director is appointed. Majority voting gives shareholders more power to control the composition of the board, even in the absence of an alternative slate. In 2010, more than two-thirds of companies in the S&P 500 had adopted majority voting for director elections—a percentage that has been increasing in recent years.[26]

The third variation is **cumulative voting**. Cumulative voting allows a shareholder to concentrate votes on a single board candidate instead of requiring one vote for each candidate. A shareholder is given a number of votes equal to the product of the number of shares owned times the number of seats the company has on its board. For example, a shareholder with 100 shares in a company with a board of nine directors has 900 votes. The shareholder can allocate those votes among board candidates as he or she chooses. To increase the chances of electing a specific director, the shareholder might concentrate more votes toward a single candidate or a subset of candidates. Cumulative voting is relatively rare. Fewer than 10 percent of companies in the S&P 500 have adopted cumulative voting (less than 1 percent for the broader university of U.S. corporations; cumulative voting is almost nonexistent in smaller companies).[27]

In the ordinary course, board elections are uncontested. The company puts up a slate of directors for election, and the shareholders are expected to elect the slate. **Contested elections** occur in two circumstances. First, in the case of a hostile takeover battle, the bidding firm puts up a full slate of directors that is sympathetic to the acquisition. If the target shareholders elect the bidder's slate, those directors will remove impediments to the takeover (such as a poison pill) and vote in favor of the deal. The second context in which contested elections take place involves an activist investor who is dissatisfied with management and wants to gain influence over the company. In this situation, the shareholder might put up a "short slate" of directors—a limited number of directors who, if elected, would constitute a minority of the board. These directors would then serve as a vehicle through which the activist investor could participate in board-level decisions. Historically, the cost of nominating a dissident slate was borne entirely by the hostile bidder or activist. For this reason, proxy contests unrelated to takeovers have been quite rare. According to the NACD, only 45 proxy contests occurred in 2008.[28]

The Dodd–Frank Financial Reform Act now stipulates that investors or groups of investors that own at least 3 percent of the company's shares continuously for three years are eligible to nominate up to 25 percent of the board. This right is known as proxy access. Importantly, these board candidates are listed on the proxy, with the cost of the contested election borne by the company. Assuming that the Dodd–Frank Act survives legal challenges, it is not yet clear how proxy access will impact the frequency of contested elections in an activist setting.

Removal of Directors

Once elected, directors generally serve their full term—one year for annually elected boards and three years for staggered boards. Shareholders may be able to prevent directors from being reelected at the next election by withholding votes. Their ability to do so, however, depends on the voting procedures in place. They can also replace directors at the next election if a competing slate of nominees is put up for election. Finally, unless a company's certificate of incorporation provides otherwise, shareholders may vote to "remove" a director between meetings. That said, shareholder power to remove a director is generally limited.

Legal Obligations of Directors

In the United States, state corporate law and federal securities law set forth the legal duties of the board. The state law applicable to a corporation is the law of the state in which the company is incorporated. A company may incorporate in any state, regardless of where its headquarters are located or where it does business. Delaware is by far the most common state of incorporation. Delaware has the most developed body of case law, which gives companies greater clarity on how corporate governance and liability matters might be decided.

Under state corporate law, the primary duties of the board are embodied in the broad principle of **fiduciary duty**. Under federal securities law, the directors' duties stem from the corporation's obligation to disclose material information to the public.

Fiduciary Duty

Under state corporate law, the board of directors has a legal obligation to act in the "interest of the corporation."[29] In legal terminology, this is referred to as a fiduciary duty to the corporation. Although somewhat ambiguous—since a corporation is simply a legal construct that cannot have its own interests—the courts have interpreted this phrase to mean that a director is expected to act in the interest of shareholders. Indeed, court decisions often refer to a fiduciary duty to "the corporation and the shareholders" or even just to the shareholders.

The fiduciary duty of the board includes three components:

- A duty of care
- A duty of loyalty
- A duty of candor

The **duty of care** requires that a director make decisions with due deliberation. In the United States, courts enforce the duty of care through the rubric of the "business judgment rule." This rule provides that the judgment of a board will not be overridden by a court unless a plaintiff can show that the board failed to inform itself regarding the decision at issue or that the board was infected with a conflict of interest, in which case there may have been a violation of the duty of loyalty. Courts have rarely ruled against a board for a violation of the duty of care. Even if a board decision was clearly wrong, if the board can show that it engaged in some consideration of information related to the decision, the courts will adopt a hands-off posture. The business judgment rule is most protective of outside directors. In the absence of "red flags" regarding what management is telling them, they are permitted to rely on what they hear from management to inform their decision. Moreover, companies are permitted to include exculpatory provisions in the charters that protect an outside director from suits for monetary damages for breach of the duty of care, so long as the director has not acted intentionally or in bad faith.

The **duty of loyalty** addresses conflicts of interest. For example, if management is considering a transaction with a company in which a director has a significant financial interest, the duty of loyalty requires that the terms of the transaction promote the interests of the shareholders over those of the director. As another example, if a director discovers a business opportunity in the course of his or her service to the company, the duty of loyalty requires that the director refrain from taking the opportunity before first determining whether the company will take it. The law lays out procedures for a board to follow in situations when a potential conflict of interest may exist.

The **duty of candor** requires that management and the board inform shareholders of all information that is important to their evaluation of the company and its management. The company's management is required in the first instance to provide accurate and timely information to shareholders, and the board is expected to oversee this process. In the absence of direct knowledge of wrongdoing, the board is permitted to rely on management assurances that the information is complete and accurate.

As a practical matter for publicly held companies, disclosure requirements mandated by federal securities law are more relevant than the duty of candor. Like the duty of candor, federal securities laws require a company and its management to disclose material information to shareholders, and that they do so in great detail. Consequently, public company shareholders are more likely to assert disclosure violations under securities laws than under the duty of candor. The duty of candor is important, however, for nonpublic companies.

Because the courts have interpreted the board's obligation to serve "in the interest of the corporation" to mean "in the interest of shareholders," corporate governance in the United States is said to be shareholder-centric. Survey data indicates that directors accept a shareholder-centric view of their responsibilities. When asked to identify in order of importance the constituents they serve, directors ranked "all shareholders" first, followed by institutional investors, customers, and creditors. They ranked other constituents such as employees and the community lower (see Table 1).[30]

Table 1 Constituents Directors Serve

Given that directors serve multiple constituencies, which are most impc	
(Listed *in order, according to director responses*)All shareholders	Given that directors serve multiple constituencies, which are most
Institutional investors	
Customers	
Creditors	
Management	
Employees	
Analysts and Wall Street	
Activist shareholders	
The community	

Source: Corporate Board Member and PricewaterhouseCoopers, LLP (2007).

In the 1990s, the legislatures of many states enacted statutes that allow the board to consider nonshareholder interests. (Delaware, where the majority of public companies are incorporated, did not adopt such a statute.) These statutes are referred to as "nonshareholder constituency" or "expanded constituency" provisions. They allow the board to consider the impact of their actions on stakeholders such as workers, customers, suppliers, and the surrounding community. The primary application of these statutes is in the evaluation of a takeover bid. These statutes purportedly allow management and the board to reject a takeover offer that is in the interest of shareholders if the takeover would harm other constituents. Still, courts generally have not allowed these statutes to be used to the disadvantage of shareholders.

According to data from SharkRepellent, approximately 10 percent of firms are incorporated in states with such a provision.[31] Ohio and Pennsylvania have gone further and *require* that the board consider nonshareholder interests. In 2010, Maryland became the first state to allow entrepreneurs to incorporate as a "benefit corporation," whereby a for-profit organization is dedicated to a specific public good, such as the environment or community involvement. This allows the company to take nonshareholder concerns into account in making decisions (see the following sidebar).

Statutes that provide for nonshareholder considerations have been litigated only to a limited extent. As a result, their meaning is still uncertain. To date, courts have interpreted them to mean that boards should take into account nonshareholder interests only to the extent that shareholder interests are not compromised. Thus, even the board of a corporation that is governed by one of these statutes has a duty to promote the interests of shareholders.

Stakeholder Interests Outside the United States

In the United Kingdom, the Companies Act 2006 allows for the consideration of nonshareholder interests in boardroom decisions. A director is required to "act in the way he considers, in good faith, would be most likely to promote the success of the company for the benefit of its members as a whole."[32] The act specifies that this includes employees, customers, suppliers, community members, the environment, creditors, and others. As this statute is relatively new in the United Kingdom, the manner in which it will be upheld is not clear.

In South Africa, governance standards are outlined in the King Report (1994), King Report II (2001), and King Report III (2009). These require that the board of directors identify all stakeholders and define the methods according to which the company promises to serve their interests. The company is expected to report financial, environmental, and social results (the so-called **triple-bottom line**), and the board of directors is expected to communicate progress against all three measures in a report to stakeholders.[33]

Disclosure Obligations Under Securities Laws

Directors have legal obligations under federal securities laws as well as state corporate laws. Federal securities laws require companies to disclose information to the public through filings with the SEC. Financial transparency improves the efficiency of capital markets by facilitating the flow of information needed for rational decision making.) SEC filings fall into three categories: filings made when a company issues securities; annual and quarterly filings; and filings upon the occurrence of transactions or events, such as a merger, a change in auditor, or the hiring of a CEO. SEC regulations specify in considerable detail the information that each of these filings must disclose. For example, the annual Form 10-K must contain a description of the company's business, risk factors, financial results by management, audited financial statements and footnotes, and compensation practices. In each filing, the company is required to include all **material information**, which is defined as information that an investor would consider important to an investment decision.

A failure to comply with these rules—by misstating material information or by omitting information and thereby making the information provided materially incorrect—exposes the company, its managers, and its directors to liability. Directors are expected to question management regarding the rationale for its disclosure decisions but, absent any red flags, they are not expected to verify information on their own.

Legal Enforcement of State Corporate Law (Fiduciary Duties)

Fiduciary duties under state corporate law are enforced through two types of judicial intervention. First, a court can issue an **injunction**, an order that the company take or refrain from taking a specified action. For example, the injunction might order that the company refrain from consummating a pending merger and allow other parties to bid. A judge might make this ruling if he or she believes that management and the board did not take all steps necessary to obtain the best deal for shareholders. Second, a court can require management and/or the directors to pay **damages** for losses sustained as a result of violating their duties.

When shareholders file suits alleging that directors have taken an action that violated their fiduciary duties, courts use different standards to review the action, depending on the nature of the alleged violation. As explained earlier, when a violation of the duty of care is involved, the courts apply the **business judgment rule**, which is most deferential to the board's decision. Under the business judgment rule, a court will not second guess a board's decision—even if, in retrospect, it was proved to be seriously deficient—if the board followed a reasonable process by which it informed itself of key, relevant facts and then made the decision in good faith. (**Good faith** requires that the board act without conflicting interests and that it not turn a blind eye to issues within its responsibility.) If the board can demonstrate that it satisfied these criteria, the courts will not intervene.

The *Disney* case is a recent high-water (or perhaps *low-water*) mark for nonintervention by the Delaware courts. In 2005, shareholders filed a derivative lawsuit against the Walt Disney Company in which they claimed that the directors did not sufficiently review the appointment of Michael Ovitz as president of the company in 1995 or his no-fault termination 14 months later. They sought to void his original employment agreement or, alternatively, to change his termination to "with cause," which under the agreement would mean the return of nearly $140 million in severance payments. Although the court agreed with the plaintiffs that the board's handling of the matter was seriously deficient, it nonetheless ruled that the business judgment rule protected the board's conduct and declined to intervene.

On the other hand, if a plaintiff successfully shows that a director has violated the duty of loyalty by virtue of a conflict of interest, the courts will not hesitate to intervene. The courts will apply a strict standard of review under which they make their own judgment whether the director has placed his or her own interest above those of shareholders. In such a case, the burden shifts to directors to demonstrate the fairness of their decision.

A board's decision to sell a company also receives a higher level of scrutiny by the courts. Because management self-interest may taint its decision to sell the company and, if so, to whom, the courts spend more time ensuring that the sale and process by which it was conducted were in the best interest of shareholders.

Legal Enforcement of Federal Securities Laws

As stated, a securities law violation stems from a material misstatement or omission of information to the public. Unless a public offering is involved, management or the directors will be held liable only if they acted intentionally or with a degree of recklessness that approaches intentionality. Importantly, the court must find that the misstatement was the cause of the investors' loss. Securities laws are stricter when a misstatement occurs in the context of a public offering. In this context, an individual can be held liable based on negligence.

Securities laws are enforced through both private lawsuits and SEC enforcement actions. Private lawsuits take the form of class actions by investors who bought (or sold) a security during the period in which its price was artificially high (or low) as a result of a material misstatement. Because it is difficult for investors to coordinate their efforts, the law allows lawyers to sue in the name of a class of investors who have suffered from a common alleged violation. Although U.S. Congress enacted reforms to the securities class action system in 1996 to facilitate a degree of oversight by institutional investors and lessen the influence of plaintiff's lawyers, plaintiff's lawyers remain largely in control of these lawsuits.

In a securities class action lawsuit, the plantiff's lawyers typically name the company and its CEO as defendants. In cases involving financial misstatements, the CFO is typically named as well. Outside board members are named much less frequently.

In an SEC enforcement action, the SEC targets members of management who were responsible for a violation. Managers are subject to monetary penalties and can be barred from serving as an officer or director of a public company, either for a specified number of years or permanently. The SEC occasionally imposes monetary penalties on companies as well. It is very unusual, however, for the SEC to target outside directors.

Director Indemnification and D&O Insurance

State corporate law and federal securities laws create some risk of liability for board members, but two mechanisms reduce the actual danger that directors make out-of-pocket payments: indemnification agreements and the purchase of directors' and officers' (D&O) liability insurance.

A company may indemnify directors for costs associated with securities class actions and some fiduciary duty cases. Indemnification generally is available to an individual director for any expense incurred in connection with litigation, including legal fees, settlements, and judgments against the director. Indemnification is only permitted, however, if the director has acted in good faith. Indemnification agreements have been widely adopted by most public companies. According to one study, 98 percent of a sample of Fortune 500 companies have indemnification arrangements for the benefit of their directors.[34]

Corporations also protect directors by purchasing **director and officer liability insurance (or D&O insurance)**. These policies cover litigation expenses, settlement payments, and, in rare cases, amounts paid in damages (up to a limit specified in the policy). A D&O insurance policy has three parts, referred to as Side A, Side B, and Side C. **Side A** protects the directors when indemnification is not available, for example, if the company becomes insolvent. **Side B** reimburses a corporation for its indemnification obligations to its directors. **Side C** insurance reimburses a corporation for its own litigation expenses and amounts it pays in settlement. As the name implies, D&O insurance contracts cover both a company's directors and officers.

D&O insurance contracts are written broadly and are intended to apply when directors are sued in private action for violating securities fraud. However, as with all insurance policies, D&O insurance has limits. First, they contain dollar limits on the coverage they provide. Amounts owed in excess of coverage limits must be paid by the company. Second, they contain exclusions. The most important of these arises when the director has committed "deliberate fraud" or otherwise illegally enriched him or herself. Third, although D&O insurance covers litigation expenses and some costs of responding to an SEC investigation that precedes litigation, it does not cover civil fines levied by the SEC (see the following sidebar).

D&O Claims and Payments

Most public attention is on high-level liabilities, such as securities violations. However, according to data from Towers Watson, a significant number of D&O claims are for other infractions, such as discrimination, wrongful termination, and contract disputes (see Table 2).

Table 2 D&O Claims and Payments

Source of Claim	Example of Allegations	% of All Claims	Average Payment	Average Defense Cost
Employees	Wrongful termination, discrimination, wage disputes	33%	$146,078	$158,698
Competitors, suppliers, and contractors	Contract disputes, business interference, copyright infringement	8%	$87,000	$420,026
Customers	Contract disputes, false advertising, deceptive trade practices	3%	—	$809,701
Government, agencies, and other third parties	Breach of fiduciary duty, false advertising, dishonesty, antitrust	16%	$13,818,125	$3,768,747
Shareholders	Inadequate disclosure, breach of fiduciary duty, stock offerings	40%	$26,456,948	$3,042,159

Source: Towers Watson, "Directors and Officers Liability: 2007 Survey of Insurance Purchasing and Claim Trends" (2007).

Despite the protections afforded to directors through indemnifications and D&O insurance, most directors believe they are at legal risk by serving on the board. When polled, more than two-thirds believe that the liability risk of serving on boards has increased in recent years. Almost 15 percent have thought seriously about resigning due to concerns about personal liability.[35] Notwithstanding this perception, the actual risk of out-of pocket payment is quite low. Black, Cheffens, and Klausner (2006) found that between 1980 and 2005, outside directors made out-of-pocket payments—meaning unindemnified and uninsured—in only 12 cases.[36] This figure includes cases where directors only incurred out-of-pocket litigation expenses and did not incur settlement costs (see Table 3).

Although indemnification and D&O insurance afford directors considerable financial protection, they do not reimburse directors for the emotional cost of the litigation process, the time involved, and the adverse impact the lawsuits might have on their reputations.[37]

Table 3 Settlements in Which Outside Directors Made Out-of-Pocket Payments (1980–2005)

	Settlement Payment	Litigation Expenses	Payment and Expenses	Total
Securities Suits under Section 10		2		2
Securities Suits That Included Section 11 Claims	4	1	1	6
SEC Enforcement Actions	1			1
Corporate Lawsuits	3			3
Total	**8**	**3**	**1**	**12**

Source: Black, Cheffens, and Klausner (2006).

Endnotes

1. The Organization for Economic Cooperation and Development, "OECD Principles of Corporate Governance. Directorate for Financial and Enterprise Affairs" (2004). Accessed July 22, 2008. See www.oecd.org/dataoecd/32/18/31557724.pdf.

2. Corporate Board Member and PricewaterhouseCoopers LLP, "What Directors Think 2009: Annual Board of Directors Survey. A Corporate Board Member Magazine/PricewaterhouseCoopers LLP Research Study. Special Supplement," *Corporate Board Member Magazine* (2009): 1-16. Accessed January 21, 2010. See www.boardmember.com/WorkArea/DownloadAsset.aspx?id=4481.

3. Corporate Board Member & PricewaterhouseCoopers LLP, "What Directors Think 2008: The Corporate Board Member/PricewaterhouseCoopers LLP Survey," *Corporate Board Member Magazine* (2008). Accessed January 21, 2010. See www.boardmember.com/Article_Details.aspx?id=1411.

4. Jay W. Lorsch, Joseph L. Bower, Clayton S. Rose, and Suraj Srinivasan, "Perspectives from the Boardroom—2009," *Harvard Business School Working Knowledge* (September 9, 2009): 1-20. Accessed January 21, 2010. See http://hbswk.hbs.edu/item/6281.html.

5. Corporate Board Member and PricewaterhouseCoopers LLP (2009).

6. *Ibid.*

7. Deloitte Touche Tohmatsu, "In the Dark: What Boards and Executives Don't Know About the Health of Their Businesses. A Survey by Deloitte in Cooperation with the Economist Intelligence Unit" (2004). Accessed September 2, 2008. See www.deloitte.com/dtt/article/0,1002,cid%253D157828,00.html.

8. Jay W. Lorsch, Joseph L. Bower, Clayton S. Rose, and Suraj Srinivasan.

9. AICPA, *The AICPA Audit Committee Toolkit* (New York: American Institute of Certified Public Accountants, 2004).

10. National Association of Corporate Directors, *2009 NACD Public Company Governance Survey* (Washington, D.C.: National Association of Corporate Directors, 2009).

11. Corporate Board Member and PricewaterhouseCoopers LLP (2009).

12. New York Stock Exchange, NYSE Listed Company Manual §303A.00, Corporate Governance Standards. See www.nyse.com/Frameset.html?nyseref=http%3A//www.nyse.com/regulation/listed/1182508124422.html&displayPage=/lcm/lcm_section.html.

13. National Association of Corporate Directors.

14. Corporate Board Member and PricewaterhouseCoopers LLP (2009).

15. New York Stock Exchange.

16. National Association of Corporate Directors.

17. Spencer Stuart "Spencer Stuart U.S. Board Index 2008" (2008). Accessed May 4, 2010. See http://content.spencerstuart.com/sswebsite/pdf/lib/SSBI_08.pdf.

18. Merck & Co., Inc., Form DEF 14A, filed with the Securities and Exchange Commission March 10, 2008.

19. Fifth Third Bancorp, Form DEF 14A, filed with the Securities and Exchange Commission March 6, 2008.

20. Cisco Systems, Inc., Form DEF 14A, filed with the Securities and Exchange Commission September 26, 2007.

21. General Mills, Inc., Form DEF 14A, filed with the Securities and Exchange Commission August 12, 2008.

22. Robert M. Daines and Michael Klausner "Do IPO Charters Maximize Firm Value? Antitakeover Protection in IPOs," *Journal of Law, Economics & Organization* 17 (2001): 83–120; John C. Coates, "Explaining Variation in Takeover Defenses: Blame the Lawyers," *California Law Review* 89 (2001): 1,301.

23. In the first half of 2009, there were 76 proposals to destagger the board. Source: National Association of Corporate Directors.

24. These descriptive statistics were generated from data supplied by SharkRepellent, FactSet Research Systems, Inc. The sample used 3,875 firms in 2009 sample and 2,849 firms in 2002.

25. Scott Smart, Chad Zutter, and Ramabhadran Thirumalai. "Why Dual-Class Shares Don't Add Up," *Directorship* 33 (2007): 14–15.

26. ISS, "Preparing for the Dodd–Frank Act" (2010). Accessed November 5, 2010. See www.issgovernance.com/weekly/20100723DoddFrank.

27. ISS Governance Analytics, *U.S. Proxy Voting Manual,* Chapter 3, "Proxy Contests, Cumulative Voting." Accessed November 5, 2010. See http://governance-analytics.com/content/menutop/content/subscription/usvmfiles/x1616.html. Descriptive statistics were generated from data supplied by SharkRepellent, FactSet Research Systems, Inc. The sample used 3,875 firms in 2009.

28. National Association of Corporate Directors.

29. See Joseph Hinsey IV, "Business Judgment and The American Law Institute's Corporate Governance Project: The Rule, the Doctrine, and the Reality," *George Washington Law Review* 52 (1984): 609–610.

30. Interestingly enough, directors apparently do not view "activist shareholders" as included in the group "all shareholders," given their disparate rankings. This implies that directors do not see themselves as serving all shareholders equally. Corporate Board Member and PricewaterhouseCoopers LLP (2007).

31. Descriptive statistics were generated from data supplied by SharkRepellent, FactSet Research Systems, Inc. The sample used 3,875 firms in 2009.

32. U.K. Companies Act of 2006 (c. 46), Part 10—A company's directors Chapter 2—General duties of directors Section 172 (1).

33. Dr. Janette Minnaar-van Veijeren, "The King II Report on Corporate Governance," i-Value Risk Management (PTY), Ltd. Accessed November 8, 2010. See www.i-value.co.za/king.html.

34. Lawrence A. Hamermesh, "Why I Do Not Teach Van Gorkom," *Georgia Law Review 34* (2000): 477–490.

35. Corporate Board Member and PricewaterhouseCoopers LLP (2009).

36. Three of the cases are quite well known: Enron ($13 million for misleading statements and $1.5 million for violating ERISA), WorldCom ($24.75 million for misleading statements), and Tyco ($22.5 million from an SEC enforcement action). The fact that these high-profile cases resulted in out-of-pocket payments no doubt contributes to the perception that a director's risk of liability has increased. See Bernard S. Black, Brian R. Cheffens, and Michael Klausner, "Outside Director Liability," *Stanford Law Review* 58 (2006): 1,055–1,159.

37. Helland (2006) finds that board member reputation generally does not suffer following allegations of fraud and that the majority of directors named in such lawsuits do not experience a decrease in board seats. An exception arises for directors named in SEC-initiated cases and those named in class actions that end in large settlements. In these cases, director reputation does suffer. Fich and Shivdasani (2007) also found that outside directors named in class-action lawsuits experience a decrease in board seats. See Eric A. Helland, "Reputational Penalties and the Merits of Class Action Securities Litigation," *Journal of Law and Economics* 49 (October 2006): 365–395. Accessed February 24, 2011. Eliezer M. Fich and Anil Shivdasani, "Financial Fraud, Director Reputation, and Shareholder Wealth" *Journal of Financial Economics* 86 (2007): 306–336.

Nathan Johnson's Rental Car Reimbursement

Should He Pocket the Cash?

Mark S. Beasley · Frank A. Buckless · Steven M. Glover · Douglas F. Prawitt

LEARNING OBJECTIVES

After completing and discussing this case you should be able to

[1] Understand ethical considerations that can arise during recruiting and in practice

[2] Reason through alternative courses of action when dealing with these issues

BACKGROUND

Nathan recently interviewed with one of the accounting firms in the city where he wants to live. The firm agreed to cover the expense of a rental car that he used to travel from his university to the firm's office. The rental car agency required that Nathan pay for the car with his credit card and have the firm reimburse Nathan for the expense rather than have the firm pay the expense directly. At the end of his trip, Nathan was supposed to pay the bill and then send the receipt to the firm for reimbursement.

As Nathan prepared to send in the receipt, he noticed that the car rental agency had overbilled him by $75. Nathan called the accounting firm to explain that his reimbursement request would be delayed because he had been overbilled. During his phone conversation with the human resource (HR) manager, Nathan told her he would call the rental agency to have his bill corrected and then would send the firm a copy for reimbursement when the revised bill arrived. The HR manager told Nathan not to bother correcting the overbilling; she suggested that he simply send in the current receipt and the firm would reimburse him for the entire amount. The HR manager was not concerned about paying the higher bill—apparently it did not meet the firm's "materiality threshold."

Before deciding whether to send in the incorrect bill, Nathan called the rental car agency to see why he was overbilled. The agent was quite rude, essentially telling Nathan to "get lost." Now Nathan was determined to get the money back, and after several long-distance phone calls and considerable hassle, the rental car company agreed to credit his card to correct the $75 overbilling. The credit will show up on Nathan's next credit card statement.

The HR manager, however, has already told Nathan that the accounting firm would pay the higher amount and requested that he not worry about the error and just send the bill in for reimbursement. Nathan immediately realized he could have the rental agency credit his card for the $75, but send the current receipt to the accounting firm to get reimbursed for the amount he originally paid. Essentially he would walk away from the deal with $75 in his pocket. Given the two hours he had spent fighting with the rental car company, a little reimbursement for his trouble didn't sound too bad to Nathan.

The case was prepared by Mark S. Beasley, Ph.D. and Frank A. Buckless, Ph.D. of North Carolina State University and Steven M. Glover, Ph.D. and Douglas F. Prawitt, Ph.D. of Brigham Young University, as a basis for class discussion. All characters and names represented are fictitious; any similarity to existing companies or persons is purely coincidental.

REQUIRED

[1] Given that the firm did not have any problem paying the higher bill, would Nathan's planned course of action be ethical? Why or why not?

[2] What other courses of action might be available to Nathan? Which do you think would be the best action for him to take?

PROFESSIONAL JUDGMENT QUESTION

[3] How might the confirmation tendency affect Nathan's decision and what could he do to mitigate the possible effects of this tendency in order to improve his professional judgment?

Anne Aylor, Inc.
Determination of Planning Materiality and Performance Materiality

Mark S. Beasley · Frank A. Buckless · Steven M. Glover · Douglas F. Prawitt

LEARNING OBJECTIVES

After completing and discussing this case you should be able to

[1] Determine planning materiality for an audit client

[2] Provide support for your materiality decisions

[3] Allocate planning materiality to financial statement elements

INTRODUCTION

Anne Aylor, Inc. (Anne Aylor) is a leading national specialty retailer of high-quality women's apparel, shoes, and accessories sold primarily under the "Anne Aylor" brand name. Anne Aylor is a highly recognized national brand that defines a distinct fashion point of view. Anne Aylor merchandise represents classic styles, updated to reflect current fashion trends. Company stores offer a full range of career and casual separates, dresses, tops, weekend wear, shoes and accessories coordinated as part of a total wardrobing strategy. The company places a significant emphasis on customer service. Company sales associates are trained to assist customers in merchandise selection and wardrobe coordination, helping them achieve the "Anne Aylor" look while maintaining the customers' personal styles.

The company follows the standard fiscal year of the retail industry, which is a 52- or 53-week period ending on the Saturday closest to January 31 of the following year. Net revenue for the year ended February 1, 2014 (referred to as fiscal 2014) was $1.2 billion and net income was $50.8 million.

At the end of fiscal 2014, the company operated approximately 584 retail stores located in 46 states under the name Anne Aylor. The company's core business focuses on relatively affluent, fashion-conscious professional women with limited shopping time. Substantially all of the company's merchandise is developed in-house by its product design and development teams. Production of merchandise is sourced to 131 independent manufacturers located in 19 countries. Approximately 45 percent, 16 percent, 13 percent, 12 percent, and 9 percent of the company's merchandise is manufactured in China, Philippines, Indonesia, India, and Vietnam, respectively. Merchandise is distributed to the company's retail stores through a single distribution center, located in Louisville, Kentucky.

Anne Aylor stock trades on The New York Stock Exchange and Anne Aylor is required to have an integrated audit of its consolidated financial statements and its internal control over financial reporting in accordance with the standards of the Public Company Accounting Oversight Board (United States). As of the close of business on March 14, 2014 Anne Aylor had 48,879,663 shares of common stock outstanding with a trading price of $22.57.

The case was prepared by Mark S. Beasley, Ph.D. and Frank A. Buckless, Ph.D. of North Carolina State University and Steven M. Glover, Ph.D. and Douglas F. Prawitt, Ph.D. of Brigham Young University, as a basis for class discussion. Anne Aylor, Inc. is a fictitious company. All characters and names represented are fictitious; any similarity to existing companies or persons is purely coincidental.

BACKGROUND

Your firm, Smith and Jones, PA., is in the initial planning phase for the fiscal 2015 audit of Anne Aylor, Inc. (i.e., the audit for the year that will end on January 31, 2015). As the audit manager, you have been assigned responsibility for determining planning materiality and performance materiality for key financial statement accounts. Your firm's materiality and performance materiality guidelines have been provided to assist you with this assignment (see Exhibit 1).

Donna Fontain, the audit partner, has performed a preliminary analysis of the company and its performance and believes the likelihood of management fraud is low. Donna's initial analysis of the company's performance is documented in the memo referenced as *G-3* (top right hand corner of the document). Additionally, Donna has documented current events/issues noted while performing the preliminary analysis in a separate memo, *G-4*. You have recorded the audited fiscal 2014 and projected fiscal 2015 financial statement numbers on audit schedule *G-7*. The company's accounting policies are provided in Exhibit 2. Assume no material misstatements were discovered during the fiscal 2014 audit.

REQUIRED

[1] Review Exhibits 1 and 2; audit memos *G-3* and *G-4;* and audit schedules *G-5, G-6* and *G-7*. Based on your review, answer each of the following questions:

- **[a]** Why are different materiality bases considered when determining planning materiality?
- **[b]** Why are different materiality thresholds relevant for different audit engagements?
- **[c]** Why is the materiality base that results in the smallest threshold generally used for planning purposes?
- **[d]** Why is the risk of management fraud considered when determining performance materiality?
- **[e]** Why might an auditor not use the same performance materiality amount or percentage of account balance for all financial statement accounts?
- **[f]** Why does the combined total of individual account performance materiality commonly exceed the estimate of planning materiality?
- **[g]** Why might certain trial balance amounts be projected when considering planning materiality?

[2] Based on your review of the Exhibits (1 and 2) and audit memos (*G-3* and *G-4*), complete audit schedules *G-5, G-6* and *G-7*.

EXHIBIT 1

Smith and Jones, PA.
Policy Statement: Planning Materiality

This policy statement provides general guidelines for firm personnel when establishing planning materiality and performance materiality for purposes of determining the nature, timing, and extent of audit procedures. The intent of this policy statement is not to suggest that these materiality guidelines must be followed on all audit engagements. The appropriateness of these materiality guidelines must be determined on an engagement by engagement basis, using professional judgment.

Planning Materiality Guidelines

Planning materiality represents the maximum, combined financial statement misstatement or omission that could occur before influencing the decisions of reasonable individuals relying on the financial statements. The magnitude and nature of financial statement misstatements or omissions will not have the same influence on all financial statement users. For example, a 5 percent misstatement with current assets may be more relevant for a creditor than a stockholder, while a 5 percent misstatement with net income before income taxes may be more relevant for a stockholder than a creditor. Therefore, the primary consideration when determining materiality is the expected users of the financial statements.

Relevant financial statement elements and presumptions on the effect of combined misstatements or omissions that would be considered immaterial and material are provided below:

- **Net Income Before Income Taxes** – combined misstatements or omissions less than 2 percent of Net Income Before Income Taxes are presumed to be immaterial and combined misstatements or omissions greater than 7 percent are presumed to be material. (Note: Net Income Before Income Taxes may not be an appropriate base if the client's Net Income Before Income Taxes is substantially below other companies of equal size or is highly variable.)
- **Net Revenue** – combined misstatements or omissions less than 0.5 percent of Net Revenue are presumed to be immaterial, and combined misstatements or omissions greater than 2 percent are presumed to be material.
- **Current Assets** – combined misstatements or omissions less than 2 percent of Current Assets are presumed to be immaterial, and combined misstatements or omissions greater than 7 percent are presumed to be material.
- **Current Liabilities** – combined misstatements or omissions less than 2 percent of Current Liabilities are presumed to be immaterial and combined misstatements or omissions greater than 7 percent are presumed to be material.
- **Total Assets** – combined misstatements or omissions less than 0.5 percent of Total Assets are presumed to be immaterial, and combined misstatements or omissions greater than 2 percent are presumed to be material. (Note: Total Assets may not be an appropriate base for service organizations or other organizations that have few operating assets.)

The specific amounts established for each financial statement element must be determined by considering the primary users as well as qualitative factors. For example, if the client is close to violating the minimum current ratio requirement for a loan agreement, a smaller planning materiality amount should be used for current assets and liabilities. Conversely, if the client is substantially above the minimum current ratio requirement for a loan agreement, it would be reasonable to use a higher planning materiality amount for current assets and current liabilities.

Planning materiality should be based on the smallest amount established from relevant materiality bases to provide reasonable assurance that the financial statements, taken as a whole, are not materially misstated for any user.

Performance Materiality Guidelines

In addition to establishing materiality for the overall financial statements, materiality for individual financial statement accounts should be established. The amount established for individual accounts is referred to as "performance materiality." Performance materiality represents the amount individual financial statement accounts can differ from their true amount without affecting the fair presentation of the financial statements taken as a whole. Establishment of performance materiality for particular accounts enables the auditor to design and execute an audit strategy for each audit cycle.

The objective in setting performance materiality for particular financial statement accounts is to provide reasonable assurance that the financial statements taken as a whole are fairly presented in all material respects.

To provide reasonable assurance that the financial statements taken as a whole do not contain material misstatements, the performance materiality established for particular financial statement accounts/transactions should not exceed 75 percent of planning materiality. The percentage threshold should be lower as the expectation for management fraud increases. In many audits it is reasonable to expect that individual financial statement account misstatements identified will be less than performance materiality and that misstatements across accounts will offset each other (some identified misstatements will overstate net income and some identified misstatements will understate net income). This expectation is not reasonable when the likelihood of management fraud is high. If management is intentionally trying to misstate the financial statements, it is likely that misstatements will be systematically biased in one direction across accounts.

The performance materiality percentage threshold should not exceed:

- 75 percent of planning materiality if low likelihood of management fraud
- 50 percent of planning materiality if reasonably low likelihood of management fraud, and
- 25 percent of planning materiality if moderate likelihood of management fraud

Finally a lower performance materiality may be required for specific accounts because of the relevance of the account to users. Performance materiality for a specific account should not exceed that amount that would influence the decision of reasonable users.

Approved: April 24, 2012

EXHIBIT 2

Anne Aylor, Inc.
Accounting Policies

Revenue Recognition – The Company records revenue as merchandise is sold to clients. The Company's policy with respect to gift certificates and gift cards is to record revenue as they are redeemed for merchandise. Prior to their redemption, these gift certificates and gift cards are recorded as a liability. While the Company honors all gift certificates and gift cards presented for payment, management reviews unclaimed property laws to determine gift certificate and gift card balances required for escheatment to the appropriate government agency. Amounts related to shipping and handling billed to clients in a sales transaction are classified as revenue and the costs related to shipping product to clients are classified as cost of sales. A reserve for estimated returns is established when sales are recorded. The Company excludes sales taxes collected from customers from net sales in its Statement of Operations.

Cost of Sales and Selling, General and Administrative Expenses – The following table illustrates the primary costs classified in each major expense category:

Cost of Sales

- Cost of merchandise sold;
- Freight costs associated with moving merchandise from our suppliers to our distribution center;
- Costs associated with the movement of merchandise through customs;
- Costs associated with the fulfillment of online customer orders;
- Depreciation related to merchandise management systems;
- Sample development costs;
- Merchandise shortage; and
- Client shipping costs.

Selling, General and Administrative Expenses

- Payroll, bonus and benefit costs for retail and corporate associates;
- Design and merchandising costs;
- Occupancy costs for retail and corporate facilities;
- Depreciation related to retail and corporate assets;
- Advertising and marketing costs;
- Occupancy and other costs associated with operating our distribution center;
- Freight expenses associated with moving merchandise from our distribution center to our retail stores; and
- Legal, finance, information systems and other corporate overhead costs.

Advertising – Costs associated with the production of advertising, such as printing and other costs, as well as costs associated with communicating advertising that has been produced, such as magazine ads, are expensed when the advertising first appears in print. Costs of direct mail catalogs and postcards are fully expensed when the advertising is scheduled to first arrive in clients' homes.

Leases and Deferred Rent Obligations – Retail stores and administrative facilities are occupied under operating leases, most of which are non-cancelable. Some of the store leases grant the right to extend the term for one or two additional five-year periods under substantially the same terms and conditions as the original leases. Some store leases also contain early termination options, which can be exercised by the Company under specific conditions. Most of the store leases require payment of a specified minimum rent, plus a contingent rent based on a percentage of the store's net sales in excess of a specified threshold. In addition, most of the leases require payment of real estate taxes, insurance and certain common area and maintenance costs in addition to the future minimum lease payments. Rent expense under non-cancelable operating leases with scheduled rent increases or free rent periods is accounted for on a straight-line basis over the initial lease term beginning on the date of initial possession, which is generally when the Company enters the space and begins construction build-out. Any reasonably assured renewals are considered. The amount of the excess of straight-line rent expense over scheduled payments is recorded as a deferred liability.

Construction allowances and other such lease incentives are recorded as deferred credits, and are amortized on a straight-line basis as a reduction of rent expense beginning in the period they are deemed to be earned, which often is subsequent to the date of initial possession and generally coincides with the store opening date. The current portion of unamortized deferred lease costs and construction allowances is included in "Accrued tenancy", and the long-term portion is included in "Deferred lease costs" on the Company's Balance Sheets.

Cash and Cash Equivalents – Cash and short-term highly liquid investments with original maturity dates of 3 months or less are considered cash or cash equivalents. The Company invests excess cash primarily in money market accounts and short-term commercial paper.

Merchandise Inventories – Merchandise inventories are valued at the lower of average cost or market, at the individual item level. Market is determined based on the estimated net realizable value, which is generally the merchandise selling price. Merchandise inventory levels are monitored to identify slow-moving items and broken assortments (items no longer in stock in a sufficient range of sizes) and markdowns are used to clear such merchandise. Merchandise inventory value is reduced if the selling price is marked below cost. Physical inventory counts are performed annually in January, and estimates are made for any shortage between the date of the physical inventory count and the balance sheet date.

Store Pre-Opening Costs – Non-capital expenditures, such as rent, advertising and payroll costs incurred prior to the opening of a new store are charged to expense in the period they are incurred.

Property and Equipment – Property and equipment are recorded at cost. Depreciation and amortization are computed on a straight-line basis over the following estimated useful lives:

Building...40 years

Leasehold improvements ....10 years or term of lease, if shorter

Furniture, fixtures and equipment.................................2-10 years

Software ....5 years

Accounting for the Impairment or Disposal of Long-Lived Assets – The assessment of possible impairment is based on the Company's ability to recover the carrying value of the long-lived asset from the expected future pre-tax cash flows (undiscounted and without interest charges). If these cash flows are less than the carrying value of such assets, an impairment loss is recognized for the difference between estimated fair value and carrying value. The primary measure of fair value is based on discounted cash flows. The measurement of impairment requires management to make estimates of these cash flows related to long-lived assets, as well as other fair value determinations.

Goodwill and Indefinite-lived Intangible Assets – The Company performs annual impairment testing related to the carrying value of the Company's recorded goodwill and indefinite-lived intangible assets.

Deferred Financing Costs – Deferred financing costs are amortized using the effective interest method over the term of the related debt.

Self Insurance – The Company is self-insured for certain losses related to its employee point of service medical and dental plans, its workers' compensation plan and for short-term disability up to certain thresholds. Costs for self-insurance claims filed, as well as claims incurred but not reported, are accrued based on management's estimates, using information received from plan administrators, third party activities, historical analysis, and other relevant data. Costs for self-insurance claims filed and claims incurred but not reported are accrued based on known claims and historical experience.

Income Taxes – The Company accounts for income taxes using the asset and liability method. Under the asset and liability method, deferred tax assets and liabilities are recognized, and income or expense is recorded, for the estimated future tax consequences attributable to differences between the financial statement carrying amounts of existing assets and liabilities and their respective tax bases.

Treasury Stock Repurchases – The Company repurchases common stock from time to time, subject to market conditions and at prevailing market prices, through open market purchases or in privately negotiated transactions. Repurchased shares of common stock are recorded using the cost method.

Stock-based Compensation – The Company uses the modified prospective method to record stock-based compensation. The calculation of stock-based compensation expense requires the input of highly subjective assumptions, including the expected term of the stock-based awards, stock price volatility, and pre-vesting forfeitures. The Company estimates the expected life of shares granted in connection with stock-based awards using historical exercise patterns, which is assumed to be representative of future behavior. The volatility of common stock at the date of grant is estimated based on an average of the historical volatility and the implied volatility of publicly traded options on the common stock. In addition, the expected forfeiture rate is estimated and expense is only recorded for those shares expected to vest. Forfeitures are estimated based on historical experience of stock-based awards granted, exercised and cancelled, as well as considering future expected behavior.

Savings Plan – Substantially all employees of the Company and its subsidiaries who work at least 30 hours per week or who work 1,000 hours during a consecutive 12 month period are eligible to participate in the Company's 401(k) Plan. Under the plan, participants can contribute an aggregate of up to 75% of their annual earnings in any combination of pre-tax and after-tax contributions, subject to certain limitations. The Company makes a matching contribution of 100% with respect to the first 3% of each participant's contributions to the 401(k) Plan and makes a matching contribution of 50% with respect to the second 3% of each participant's contributions to the 401(k) Plan.

Other Liabilities – Other liabilities includes liabilities associated with borrowings for the purchase of fixed assets and obligation for excess corporate office space.

Anne Aylor, Inc.
Memo: Analysis of Performance First Quarter
Year Ended: January 31, 2015

Reference:	G 3
Prepared by:	DF
Date:	6/14/15
Reviewed by:	

Net sales for the first quarter of fiscal 2015 increased 1.5 percent from the first quarter of fiscal 2014. Comparable store sales for the first quarter of fiscal 2015 increased 0.5 percent, compared to a comparable store sales decrease of 0.2 percent in the first quarter of fiscal 2014. Despite soft customer traffic across the industry, the Company saw improvement in same store sales as a result of a targeted promotional strategy and improved product offerings that helped drive increased traffic to Company stores. Based on their current strategy and performance to date, the company expects to achieve net sales growth of approximately 5 percent for the 2015 fiscal year compared to 3.5 percent for fiscal 2014. Net sales growth for the company's market sector is expected to be approximately 3 percent for the 2015 fiscal year.

Gross margin as a percentage of net sales increased to 51.5 percent in the first quarter of fiscal 2015, compared to 51.0 percent in the first quarter of fiscal 2014. The increase in gross margin as a percentage of net sales for the first quarter of fiscal 2015 as compared to the comparable fiscal 2014 period was due primarily to higher full price sales as a percentage of total sales coupled with higher margin rates achieved on both full price and non-full price sales at stores. This performance was the result of improved product offerings and effective targeted marketing initiatives.

Selling, general and administrative expenses as a percentage of net sales decreased to 47.2 percent, in the first quarter of fiscal 2015, compared to 48.0 percent of net sales in the first quarter of fiscal 2014. The decrease in selling, general and administrative expenses as a percentage of net sales was primarily due to improved operating leverage as a result of higher net sales, tenancy related savings associated with the store remodel program, and continued focus on cost savings initiatives. The decrease in selling, general and administrative expenses was partially offset by higher marketing and performance-based compensation expenses.

Net income as a percentage of net sales increased to 2.6 percent in the first quarter of fiscal 2015, compared to 1.8 percent in the first quarter of fiscal 2014. The increase in net income as a percentage of net sales is due to improved full price selling at Company stores and improved operating efficiencies. Based on their current strategy and performance to date, the company expects to achieve net earnings before taxes growth of approximately 23 percent for the 2015 fiscal year compared to 18 percent for fiscal 2014.

Anne Aylor, Inc.
Memo: Current Events/Issues
Year Ended: January 31, 2015

Reference:	G 4
Prepared by:	DF
Date:	6/14/15
Reviewed by:	

The company plans to focus on optimizing store productivity and enhancing the in-store environment of existing stores. Last year the Company remodeled 4 stores with updated aesthetics and reducing the square footage 30-40%. The Company intends to remodel an additional 25 stores during fiscal 2015 following the remodeled prototype developed last year. The remodeling will be funded with operating cash flows.

On March 18, 2015 the Company entered into the credit facility with First Bank and a syndicate of lenders, which amended its existing $150 million senior secured revolving credit facility which was due to expire in October 2015. The credit facility provides the Company with an option to increase the total facility and the aggregate commitments thereunder up to $200 million, subject to the lenders' agreement to increase their commitment for the requested amount. The credit facility expires on September 30, 2020 and may be used for working capital, letters of credit and other general corporate purposes. Should certain liquidity and other requirements not be met, as defined in the credit facility, no additional funds can be borrowed and any outstanding borrowings may become immediately payable. The credit facility requires that the Company maintain a working capital balance of $125 million and quick ratio of 0.65. Additionally, the Company is only allowed to repurchase common stock up to $100,000 in any fiscal year.

Anne Aylor, Inc.
Planning Materiality Assessment
Year Ended: January 31, 2015

Reference: *G 5*
Prepared by: ______
Date: ______
Reviewed by: ______

Primary Users of Financial Statements (list):

Materiality Bases (in thousands):

Base	Fiscal 2014 Actual Financial Statement Amounts	Fiscal 2015 Projected Financial Statement Amounts	Planning Materiality Levels			
			Lower Limit		Upper Limit	
			Percent	Dollar Amount	Percent	Dollar Amount
Income Before Taxes			*2*		*7*	
Net Revenues			*0.5*		*2*	
Current Liabilities			*2*		*7*	
Current Assets			*2*		*7*	
Total Assets			*0.5*		*2*	

Planning Materiality (in thousands): $

Explanation:

Anne Aylor, Inc.
Performance Materiality Assessment
Year Ended: January 31, 2015

Reference: G 6
Prepared by: ______
Date: ______
Reviewed by: ______

Likelihood of Management Fraud (check one):

______ Low Likelihood of Management Fraud
______ Reasonably Low Likelihood of Management Fraud
______ Moderate Likelihood of Management Fraud

Performance Materiality (in thousands):

Planning Materiality:	$
Multiplication Factor (0.75 if low likelihood of management fraud, 0.50 if reasonably low likelihood of management fraud, and 0.25 if moderate likelihood of management fraud).	X
Performance Materiality (in thousands)	$

Specific Accounts Requiring Lower Performance Materiality:

Account	**Performance Materiality**
Explanation:	
Explanation:	
Explanation:	
Explanation:	
Explanation:	
Explanation:	

Anne Aylor, Inc.
Planning Materiality Financial Information
Year Ended: January 31, 2015

Reference: G 7
Prepared by:
Date:
Reviewed by:

All amounts are in thousands	1/31/2015 Projected	2/1/2014 Actual
Net sales	$ 1,305,600	$ 1,243,788
Cost of sales	596,700	573,727
Gross margin	708,900	670,061
Selling, general and administrative expenses	604,600	585,225
Operating income/(loss	104,300	84,836
Interest income	700	636
Interest expense	1,100	1,009
Income/(loss) before income taxes	103,900	84,463
Income tax provision/(benefit)	41,400	33,686
Net income/(loss)	$ 62,500	$ 50,777
Assets		
Current assets		
Cash and cash equivalents	$ 124,200	$ 115,845
Accounts receivable	13,900	12,892
Merchandise inventories	148,600	137,647
Refundable income taxes	4,500	4,165
Deferred income taxes	17,900	16,572
Prepaid expenses and other current assets	38,000	35,199
Total current assets	347,100	322,320
Property and equipment, net	275,500	254,475
Deferred income taxes	4,100	3,790
Other assets	13,700	12,670
Total assets	$ 640,400	$ 593,255
Liabilities		
Current liabilities		
Accounts payable	$ 62,800	$ 58,165
Accrued salaries and bonus	27,800	25,779
Accrued tenancy	23,800	22,014
Gift certificates and merchandise credits redeemable	30,600	27,654
Accrued expenses and other current liabilities	60,200	55,768
Total current liabilities	205,200	189,380
Deferred lease costs	102,100	94,593
Deferred income taxes	-	21
Long-term performance compensation	9,600	8.877
Other liabilities	33,800	31,339
Total liabilities	350,700	324,210
Stockholders' equity		
Common stock and paid in capital	466,300	432,080
Retained earnings	483,000	447,556
Accumulated other comprehensive loss	(1,800)	(1,652)
Treasury stock	(657,800)	(608,939)
Total stockholders' equity	289,700	269,045
Total liabilities and stockholders' equity	$ 640,400	$ 593,255

Satyam Computer Services Limited

Controlling the Confirmation Process

MARK S. BEASLEY · FRANK A. BUCKLESS · STEVEN M. GLOVER · DOUGLAS F. PRAWITT

LEARNING OBJECTIVES

After completing and discussing this case you should be able to

[1] Understand common procedures used to audit cash, including proper confirmation procedures.

[2] Identify audit documentation requirements, especially once an audit is complete.

[3] Recognize consequences that can be imposed on an audit firm subsequent to a PCAOB enforcement action.

[4] Understand the SEC's oversight authority for companies that trade shares on U.S. stock exchanges as American Depositary Shares (ADS).

[5] Recognize how membership in a network of firms might impact a member accounting firm.

INTRODUCTION[1]

"It was like riding a tiger, not knowing how to get off without being eaten," according to Satyam Computer Services Limited (Satyam) former Chairman, B. Ramalinga Raju, soon after massive fraud involving the company's financial statements was revealed. For over five years, Raju was at the top of a massive fraud scheme orchestrated by senior executives at the Hyderabad, India information technology services company that falsely inflated its cash and cash-related balances by over $1 billion. In an amazing fraud scheme that went undetected by the company's external auditors, senior executives directed the creation of over 6,000 false invoices and manufactured numerous false bank statements to create over $1 billion in fictitious cash balances and other interest bearing deposits.

Just before the fraud was revealed in January 2009, Satyam's shares traded on the New York Stock Exchange (NYSE) at a price of $9.35. When trading resumed the next day, those shares dropped nearly 85 percent to close at $1.46. Institutional investors who owned those shares realized losses of over $450 million.

The audit of cash is often viewed as a fairly simple and straightforward set of procedures. Frequently, responsibility for verification of cash balances is assigned to newer, experienced members of the audit engagement team because of the relative low risk nature of cash related assertions and the objective versus subjective types of audit evidence typically examined. So, when the fraud was revealed, many were left wondering how such a massive fraud involving overstatement of cash balances went undetected by auditors for several years.

---

1 The information in this case is based on the SEC Litigation Release No. 21915/Accounting and Auditing Enforcement Release No. 3258, U.S. Securities and Exchange Commission v. Satyam Computer Services Limited d/b/a Mahindra Satyam, Civil Action No. 1:11-CV-00672 (D.D.C.), and PCAOB Release No. 105-2011-002, Order Instituting Disciplinary Proceedings, Making Findings, and Imposing Sanctions, In the Matter of Price Waterhouse, Bangalore, Lovelock & Lewes, Price Waterhouse & Co., Bangalore, Price Waterhouse, Calcutta, and Price Waterhouse & Co., Calcutta (April 5, 2011).

The case was prepared by Mark S. Beasley, Ph.D. and Frank A. Buckless, Ph.D. of North Carolina State University and Steven M. Glover, Ph.D. and Douglas F. Prawitt, Ph.D. of Brigham Young University, as a basis for class discussion. It is not intended to illustrate either effective or ineffective handling of an administrative situation.

SATYAM COMPUTER SERVICES LIMITED

Satyam was a large information technology services company with principal executive offices in Hyderabad, India. At the time of the fraud, the company employed over 50,000 individuals worldwide and maintained offices around the globe, including several in the United States. Company shares traded on the Bombay Stock Exchange, the National Stock Exchange of India, and 65 million of its American Depositary Shares (ADS) traded on the New York Stock Exchange. The ADS shares represented between 11 and 20 percent of the company's total shares outstanding. As an ADS registrant, the company filed its financial statements with the United States Securities and Exchange Commission (SEC).

The main line of business for Satyam was information technology services that it provides to a variety of customers worldwide. The company prepared and submitted invoices for the services performed to its customers and recorded those invoices in its invoice management system. Data from that system was then exported into Satyam's financial accounting system, which management used to prepare the financial statements for its March 31 fiscal year ends.

FALSIFICATION OF REVENUES AND CASH

On January 7, 2009, Satyam submitted a Form 6-K to the SEC that included a letter prepared by then-Satyam Chairman Raju admitting that the company had been engaged in a billion dollar financial fraud involving the overstatement of more than $1 billion in cash and bank balances when the actual amounts were $66 million. The overstatement of cash was tied to a fraud scheme senior management had used to overstate company revenues over the past five fiscal years ending in 2004-2008.

During that period, senior management falsified the company's reported revenues by creating false invoices for services never performed and for customers who never existed. To orchestrate the falsification of invoices, senior management provided certain employees with "super-user" login identification and password access to the invoice management system. The "super-user" login allowed the inclusion of false invoices to overstate revenues while also enabling the concealment of those invoices from lower-level members of management who might recognize the invoices as fake. Employees in on the fraud generated between 100 to 200 fake invoices a month, which ultimately led to the recording of over 6,600 false invoices in the invoice management system and the company's quarter and annual financial statements.

The chart below summarizes the impact of the falsification of the fictitious invoices for five and one-half years ending in 2009:

Fiscal Year	Number of False Invoices	Recorded Revenues	False Revenues
2004	267	$ 566,370,000	$ 46,410,000
2005	451	793,600,000	68,860,000
2006	1,180	1,096,300,000	149,500,000
2007	654	1,461,400,000	151,650,000
2008	2,483	2,138,100,000	430,390,000
2009	1,568	1,289,500,000	275,860,000
Total	**6,603**	**$7,345,270,000**	**$1,122,670,000**

Note: Because the fraud was revealed in the middle of 2009, the amounts reflected above for 2009 only represent misstatements for the first two quarters of the fiscal year.

As can be seen in the table above, the fraud enabled the company to overstate its revenues on a cumulative basis over the five plus years in excess of $1.1 billion, enabling the company to report net profits in periods where net income was actually less than zero. To compensate for their recording of false revenues, management buried the false entries in numerous cash accounts linked to bank accounts at six banks. Senior management concealed the scheme by preparing false bank statements to reflect cash deposits that it did not have in the company's bank accounts. As shown below, cash-related balances reported on the balance sheets at each fiscal year end were massively overstated.

Balance Sheet Date	Reported Cash and Interest	Actual Cash and Interest	Amount of Overstatement
March 31, 2004	$252,022,199	$ 4,369,680	$ 247,652,519
March 31, 2005	417,067,645	260,436	416,807,209
March 31, 2006	432,722,174	26,511,770	406,210,404
March 31, 2007	780,756,619	13,365,348	767,391,271
March 31, 2008	912,660,956	2,210,812	910,450,144
September 30, 2008	784,605,511	2,177,546	782,427,965

In addition to overstating the cash balance, management also overstated its accounts receivable balances.

THE AUDIT OF SATYAM'S FINANCIAL STATEMENTS

Price Waterhouse, Bangalore (PW Bangalore) based in Bangalore, Karnataka, India served as Satyam's independent auditor, signing the audit opinions on the financial statements of Satyam from 2000 through 2009. PW Bangalore was one of five India firms that worked closely together as part of a larger network of accounting firms known as PW India. The other four firms linked with PW Bangalore in the PW India network were: Lovelock & Lewes, Price Waterhouse & Co., Bangalore, Price Waterhouse, Calcutta, and Price Waterhouse & Co., Calcutta.[2] This network of firms shared resources under a common leadership that included the sharing of engagement personnel, office space, and telephone numbers.

While Lovelock & Lewes participated in the audits of Satyam's financial statements for the years ended 2005 through 2008, the remaining three firms in the network did not participate in any of the audits. PW Bangalore was engaged to perform the audits of the financial statements and issued unqualified audit opinions on the Satyam annual financial statements based on audits performed in accordance with PCAOB auditing standards for each of the fiscal years 2005 through 2008.

AUDIT OF CASH AND RECEIVABLES

Because reported cash represented between 50 and 60 percent of total reported assets on the balance sheets during the years 2004 through 2008, the audit engagement team sought to verify the existence and accuracy of the recorded cash balances. As part of the audit team's procedures, the engagement team signed the auditor's confirmation requests and gave the requests to employees of Satyam, who were responsible for sending the confirmation requests to the banks.

Later, Satyam employees returned the alleged completed confirmation responses from the six banks to the audit engagement team. These responses covered approximately 93 percent of Satyam's reported cash for each year end. At the same time, the engagement team separately received confirmation responses directly from other branches of the same banks. Interestingly, the bank-supplied confirmation responses reflected significantly smaller cash balances than Satyam

2 Despite having very similar names, each of these four firms are distinct firms. That is, Price Waterhouse, Calcutta, and Price Waterhouse and Co., Calcutta are different firms.

management asserted were held in fixed deposits at the same banks and significantly lower than the amounts reported on the "confirmation responses" provided to the engagement team by Satyam management. For example, in the 2008 audit, Satyam management provided a confirmation response supposedly from the Mumbai branch of a bank that indicated the company held approximately $176 million of fixed deposits with the bank. At the same time, the auditors received directly from the Hyderabad branch of the same bank a confirmation response indicating that Satyam had no fixed assets with the bank. Unfortunately, the engagement team did not perform procedures to reconcile these kinds of differences in responses.

The approach the auditors took in their audit of accounts receivable was similar to the approach the auditors took in the audit of cash. For the 2006 and 2007 audits, the engagement team relied on Satyam management to send confirmation requests for accounts receivable. Despite never receiving any responses to these confirmation requests, the engagement team made no attempt to follow-up on the non-responses with second confirmation requests.

At one point, the auditors did perform alternative procedures by verifying subsequent cash receipts. However, they never ensured that the cash received after year end related to individual invoices outstanding at year end. And, in some cases, the subsequent cash receipts testing was performed as of a date that differed from the fiscal year end date.

These audit responses also failed to take into account deficiencies they noted in Satyam controls. As part of the firm's testing of IT controls in 2007 and 2008 required by Section 404 of the Sarbanes-Oxley Act, the firm noted over 170 deficiencies in internal control, including eight significant deficiencies that indicated a heightened risk related to accounts receivable. Unfortunately, the audit firm failed to adjust its audit plan in response to these findings.

AUDIT DOCUMENTATION

To make matters worse, in November 2007, PW Bangalore and Lovelock & Lewes learned that the 2007 Satyam audit engagement would be inspected by the PCAOB in February 2008. PW Bangalore issued its audit opinion on the March 31, 2007 financial statements on April 27, 2007. Between November 2007 and the arrival of the inspectors in early 2008, members of the audit engagement team created new documents that were added to the audit working papers; however, none of the documents disclosed the dates the documents were added, the persons preparing the documents, or the reasons for adding those documents.

CHARGES AND SANCTIONS

Shortly after the fraud was revealed, the Government of India assumed control of the company and dissolved the existing board of directors, replacing them with new government-nominated directors. In February 2009, the Company Law Board of India authorized the new board of directors to seek a strategic investor for Satyam. By May 2009, an Indian information technology company, Tech Mahindra Limited, a subsidiary of Venturbay Consultants Private Limited, was selected. The new board of directors had installed new senior management team, which included executives from Tech Mahindra Limited, and announced its new brand identity as "Mahindra Satyam" by the end of June 2009. Additionally, Indian authorities filed criminal charges against several former officers.

In April 2011 the SEC announced that it had settled a civil action against the company and that the company had agreed to pay a $10 million penalty. The SEC's enforcement action also noted that Satyam must require specific training of officers and employees concerning securities laws and accounting principles and improve its internal audit function. In addition, the company agreed to hire an independent consultant to evaluate the internal controls at Satyam.

As for the auditors, the PCAOB censured all five audit firms included in the PW India network. The PCAOB also temporarily limited the activities and operations of PW India, including a prohibition from accepting SEC issuer referred engagement work for new clients for a period of six months. In addition, the PCAOB required PW India to engage an independent monitor, adopt and implement certain changes to the network of firm's quality control, and provide additional professional education and training to its personnel. Finally, the PCAOB imposed a civil monetary penalty in the amount of $1.5 million on PW Bangalore and Lovelock & Lowes.

REQUIRED

[1] Research the difference between American Depositary Shares and American Depositary Receipts. Then, visit the SEC's website (www.sec.gov) to locate the final SEC rule Release No. 33-8879 issued on December 21, 2007 and research whether foreign issuers must file with the SEC financial statements in conformity with generally accepted accounting principles (GAAP).

[2] Research auditing standards and other guidance on effective internal control to answer the following questions:

[a] What are IT general controls and what type(s) of IT general controls were compromised in the Satyam fraud?

[b] What is meant by the term management override and how was that revealed in the Satyam fraud?

[3] Research PCAOB auditing standards (which can be found on the PCAOB's website – www.pcaob.org) related to the use of confirmations and document the specific requirements related to maintaining control of the confirmation process.

[a] Based on what you learn, provide an assessment of deficiencies in the confirmation approach Satyam's auditors took related to cash and accounts receivable.

[b] Do auditing standards require the use of confirmations in the audits of cash balances and accounts receivable balances?

[4] The Satyam auditors attempted to confirm both cash and accounts receivable balances with external parties. Which of the audit assertions for cash and accounts receivable would confirmations be most relevant?

[5] Research the PCAOB's website (www.pcaob.org) to learn about the PCAOB's inspection process. How often are firms inspected by the PCAOB and to what extent are the inspection findings available to the investing public?

[6] Research PCAOB auditing standards (which can be found on the PCAOB's website – www.pcaob.org) related to the use of audit documentation and identify specific requirements related to deadlines for including audit documentation in the engagement workpapers, such as the documentation completion date. Also, identify requirements related to what must be documented on the workpaper, including the date of preparation of audit documentation and the identification of the preparers of the documentation. Based on your findings, provide your assessment of how PW Bangalore violated these requirements.

[7] Research the AICPA's Code of Professional Conduct (which is available on the AICPA's website – www.aicpa.org) to research what it means to be in a "network" of firms. How might the actions of one of the accounting firms in the network impact other members of the network?

[8] Locate the PCAOB's Settled Disciplinary Order against the auditors of the Satyam financial statements, which can be found on the PCAOB's website under the link for "Enforcement" (see PCAOB Release No. 105-2011-002 dated April 5, 2011), and review the sanctions imposed on the audit firms within the PW India network. You will see that the PCAOB censured all five firms in the PW India network, even though three of those firms did not participate in the audit of Satyam's financial statements. Discuss why the PCAOB charged all five firms rather than only charge PW Bangalore and Lovelock & Lewes?

PROFESSIONAL JUDGMENT QUESTIONS

[9] One of the judgment shortcuts that can lead to bias in professional judgments is the "confirmation tendency." Briefly describe what is meant by confirmation tendency and where was that evident in the auditor's judgment process in the Satyam case?

[10] What can professionals do to overcome the confirmation tendency?

Going Green
Sustainability and External Reporting

Mark S. Beasley · Frank A. Buckless · Steven M. Glover · Douglas F. Prawitt

LEARNING OBJECTIVES

After completing and discussing this case you should be able to

[1] Describe the major elements that should be included in a sustainability report following the Global Reporting Initiative (GRI) framework

[2] Describe the potential advantages and disadvantages associated with sustainability reporting

[3] Describe the types of assurance services accountants can provide to clients issuing sustainability reports to external parties

[4] Describe potential advantages and disadvantages of obtaining third party assurances about corporate sustainability reports

[5] Describe major challenges for accountants who may be asked to issue an assurance report on corporate sustainability reporting

[6] Evaluate a corporate sustainability report using the GRI framework

INTRODUCTION

A 2014 Gallup Poll[1] survey regarding Americans' concerns about environmental issues revealed the following:

Tell me if you personally worry about this problem a great deal, fair amount, only a little or not at all?	Worry Great Deal/ Fair Amount	Worry Little/ Not At All
Pollution of drinking water	82%	18%
Pollution of rivers, lake and reservoirs	81%	18%
Contamination of soil and water by toxic waste	77%	22%
Air pollution	73%	28%
Extinction of plant and animal species	65%	34%
The loss of tropical rain forests	68%	33%
Climate change	60%	39%
Global warming	56%	43%

Given results of surveys like the one above, it shouldn't be surprising that more and more business leaders are concerned with how their business is impacting the environment and increasingly want to demonstrate that they are being good stewards of the environment.

1 Jones, Jeff and Lydia Saad. "Gallup Poll Social Series: Environment" *Gallup*. April 4, 2014. See the following website: http://www.gallup.com/poll/168236/americans-show-low-levels-concern-global-warming.aspx

The case was prepared by Mark S. Beasley, Ph.D. and Frank A. Buckless, Ph.D. of North Carolina State University and Steven M. Glover, Ph.D. and Douglas F. Prawitt, Ph.D. of Brigham Young University, as a basis for class discussion. It is not intended to illustrate either effective or ineffective handling of an administrative situation.

BACKGROUND

The term "sustainability" means different things to different people. A traditional view of sustainability is to "... meet society's present needs without compromising the ability of future generations to meet their own needs."[2] In this context, sustainability is concerned with meeting economic and social needs of society while minimizing negative environmental impacts. From a business perspective, sustainability is often viewed differently as the ability of a business organization to sustain its operations over the long term. From this perspective, the goal of sustainability is to create long term shareholder and social value while reducing the usage of nonrenewable resources and minimizing the negative environmental impacts. To achieve this goal, business organizations must employ practices that integrate economic, social, and environmental considerations into their decision processes.

Paying attention to sustainability issues is not just a moral issue. Why else are business organizations showing growing interest in sustainability issues? Many are realizing that creating shareholder value doesn't have to be a trade-off between economic, social, and environmental factors. Instead, shareholder value can be enhanced by capturing the synergy between economic, social, and environmental factors. Business leaders are recognizing that a focus on sustainability can create competitive advantage.

What is the business case for implementing sustainability practices? Esty and Simmons identify four potential benefits of incorporating sustainability into a business organization's strategy. Those benefits are:[3]

- Operating cost reductions and efficiency gains.
- Environmental risk reductions.
- Revenue growth.
- Intangible value growth.

Operating cost reductions and efficiency gains can be achieved by elimination or reduction of scrap, waste, energy usage, and other reduced costs through regulatory compliance (e.g., avoidance of penalties and fines). Reductions of waste and pollution emissions help mitigate environmental risks thus minimizing government fines, product recalls and diminished brand/customer loyalty. Development of products that are viewed positively from an environmental perspective can provide a business organization competitive advantage with customers who are especially focused on the impact of the business on the environment. Other intangible benefits achieved by having a strategic focus on sustainability include improved brand/customer loyalty and improved attraction, retention and productivity of employees.

A 2013 KPMG survey report of 4,100 companies across 41 countries indicates that 51 percent of the surveyed companies report sustainability information in their financial reports and 71 percent issue sustainability reports.[4] The GRI Sustainability Reporting Statistics database[5] reveals that the number of organizations issuing external sustainability reports has increased every year since 1999. In 1999, less than 100 organizations issued external sustainability reports while over 3,000 organizations issued external sustainability reports in 2013.

The GRI database also reveals that the number of organizations obtaining third-party assurance on their sustainability reports was 30 percent in 2013. Finally, this database highlights that organizations with a more comprehensive sustainability report are much more likely to obtain third party assurance on their sustainability information. The 2013 KPMG survey report highlights that 59 percent of the world's largest 250 global companies obtain external assurance on sustainability

2 U.S. Environmental Protection Agency. "Sustainability: Basic Information" See the following website: http://www.epa.gov/sustainability/basicinfo.htm#sustainability

3 Esty, Daniel C. and P. J. Simmons. "The Green to Gold Business Playbook." *John Wiley and Sons, Inc.* 2011.

4 KPMG International Cooperative. "The KPMG Survey of Corporate Responsibility Reporting 2013." December 2013. This article can be found at http://www.kpmg.com/global.

5 See the following website: http://database.globalreporting.org/pages/about and click on "GRI Reports List" to download the database.

information. As business organizations become more comfortable with measuring and reporting sustainability information, requests for assurance services on sustainability information will likely grow.

SUSTAINABILITY REPORTING GUIDELINES

Currently there is no generally accepted reporting standard for corporate sustainability reporting. The most widely used reporting guidelines for corporate sustainability reporting is the framework issued by the Global Reporting Initiative (GRI).[6] The GRI was started in 1997 by the non-profit organization "Coalition for Environmentally Responsible Economies" (CERES) based out of Boston, Massachusetts. Today the GRI is an independent organization, based out of Amsterdam, Netherlands, with the mission to "... make sustainability reporting standard practice by providing guidance and support to organizations."[7]

POTENTIAL ASSURANCE ENGAGEMENT

Several clients have approached your accounting firm, Green and Brown, LLP, about the possibility of engaging your firm to provide assurance on their sustainability report. One of the audit partners, Annette Crossland, asked you to conduct some background research on the feasibility of Green and Brown expanding its service lines to include assurances on corporate environmental and social performance reports.

REQUIRED (CONTINUED ON NEXT PAGE)

[1] Go to the Global Reporting Initiative's website (try http://www.globalreporting.org) and obtain and read the G4 Sustainability Reporting Guidelines Part 1 Reporting Principles and Standard Disclosures.

- [a] What are the major types of general standard disclosures and what type of information is included under each type of general standard disclosure?
- [b] What are the major types of specific standard disclosures and what type of information is included under each type of specific standard disclosure?
- [c] What are the major differences between the two "In Accordance" levels?

[2] Go to the Global Reporting Initiative's website (try http://www.globalreporting.org) and obtain the G4 Sustainability Reporting Guidelines Part 2 Implementation Manual and read the assurance guidance (G4-33) provided in the report profile section of the manual. The assurance guidance (G4-33) identifies seven key elements for providing assurance on sustainability reports. What are the seven key elements?

[3] Read AICPA Attestation Standard Sections 50 and 101 and go to UPS's sustainability report (try http://www.responsibility.ups.com/sustainability) to see examples of assurance reports on sustainability information. What types of engagements do the attestation standards cover? What level of assurance is allowed with the attestation standards? How do the eleven generally accepted attestation standards compare to the seven elements for providing assurance on sustainability reports as outlined in the G4 Sustainability Reporting Guidelines Part 2 Implementation Manual (G4-33)?

---

6 See the following website: http://www.globalreporting.org/Home

7 Global Reporting Initiative. "Mission." See the following website: http://www.globalreporting.org/AboutGRI/WhatIsGRI/VisionAndMission.htm

[4] Read International Standard on Assurance Engagements (ISAE) 3000. What types of engagements does ISAE 3000 cover? Would ISAE 3000 allow accountants to provide assurance on an organization's sustainability report? Explain your answer. What level of assurance is allowed with ISAE 3000? How do requirements for performing an assurance engagement using ISAE 3000 compare to the requirements for performing an assurance engagement using the AICPA Attestation Standards? How do requirements for performing an assurance engagement using ISAE 3000 compare to the requirements for performing an audit of financial statements? How do the requirements for performing an assurance engagement using ISAE 3000 compare to the seven elements for providing assurance on sustainability reports as outlined in the G4 Sustainability Reporting Guidelines Part 2 Implementation Manual (G4-33)?

[5] Based on what you have read related to sustainability reporting, what do you believe are the possible advantages and disadvantages associated with issuing a sustainability report to external stakeholders? What do you believe are the major reasons why some business organizations are reluctant to issue sustainability reports to external stakeholders?

[6] Based on what you have read related to sustainability reporting, what do you believe are the possible advantages and disadvantages associated with having a third party provide assurance on a business organization's sustainability report? What do you believe are the major reasons why some business organizations are reluctant to have third party assurance provided on their sustainability report? What are the key challenges for accountants who might be asked to issue an attestation report on a business organization's sustainability report?

[7] The GRI Sustainability Reporting Statistics database[8] indicates that 30 percent of the organizations issuing 2013 sustainability reports obtained external assurance and that the majority of the external assurance was provided by accounting firms. What are the advantages of having accounting firms as compared to other third party groups, like engineering or consulting firms providing assurance services on corporate sustainability reports? What are the advantages of having non-accounting firms like engineering or consulting firms, as compared to accounting firms providing assurance services on corporate sustainability reports?

[8] Go to Caterpillar Inc.'s website (try http://www.caterpillar.com) to locate Caterpillars' latest sustainability report. What aspect of sustainability reporting seems to be a priority for Caterpillar? Explain your answer. Based on your reading of the G4 Sustainability Reporting Guidelines what "In Accordance" level would you assign to Caterpillar's sustainability report?

[9] Go to Caterpillar Inc.'s website (try http://www.caterpillar.com) to locate Caterpillar's latest sustainability report. Go to Caterpillar Inc.'s website (try http://www.caterpillar.com) to locate Caterpillar's latest 10-K report. How consistent is the business strategy discussed in the 10-K to the sustainability strategy discussed in the sustainability report? How well does the sustainability report connect to financial information reported in the 10-K report? Do these two reports provide information on how sustainability is embedded into management processes such as human resources, purchasing, finance, etc.? Explain your answers.

[10] The GRI Sustainability Reporting database[9] reveals that approximately 12 percent of the organizations issuing 2013 sustainability reports issued integrated reports. An integrated report combines in one report information on economic, social, and environmental performance. Go to American Electric Power's website (try http://www.aepsustainability.com) to read American Electric Power's integrated report in electronic format. Based on your reading of the integrated report for American Electric Power, what are the advantages and disadvantages of a business organization issuing an integrated report instead of issuing a separate report for financial performance and sustainability performance?

---

8 See the following website: http://database.globalreporting.org/pages/about and click on "GRI Reports List" to download the database.

9 Ibid.

Index

S

T

U

V

W